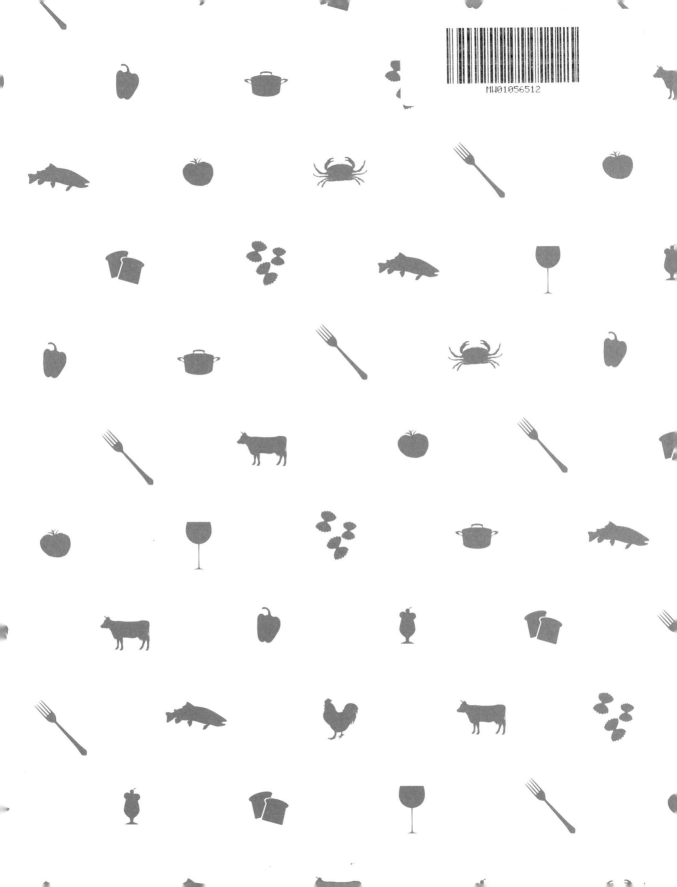

MW01056512

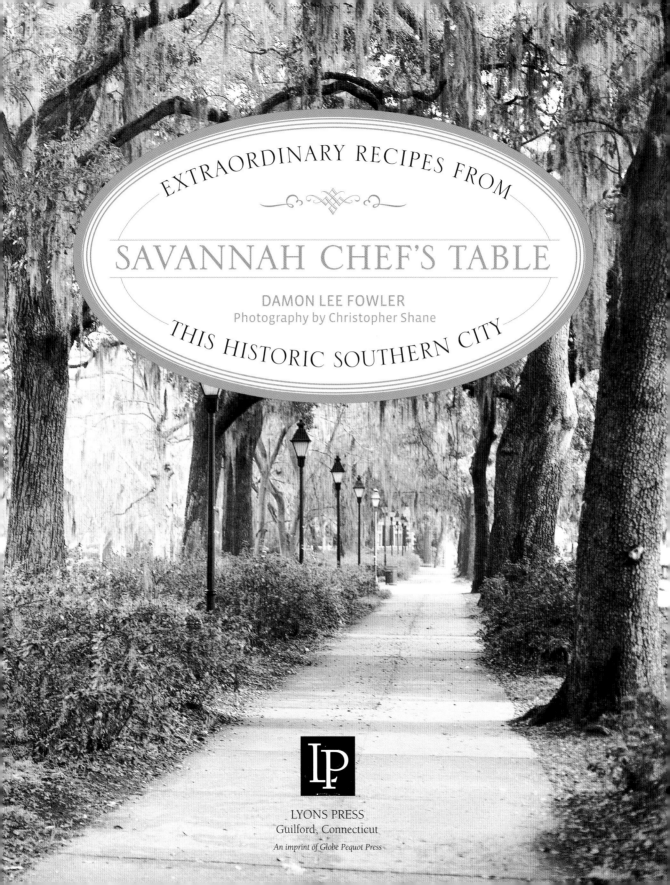

EXTRAORDINARY RECIPES FROM

SAVANNAH CHEF'S TABLE

DAMON LEE FOWLER

Photography by Christopher Shane

THIS HISTORIC SOUTHERN CITY

LYONS PRESS
Guilford, Connecticut

An imprint of Globe Pequot Press

All photographs by Christopher Shane except those on pages 53, 56–57, and 160 by Lily
Lewin, pages 165 and 167 by Tim A. Rutherford and the author photo on page 188 by Timothy
Hall

Editor: Katie Benoit
Project Editor: Tracee Williams
Text Design: Libby Kingsbury
Layout Artist: Nancy Freeborn

Library of Congress Cataloging-in-Publication Data is available on file.

ISBN 978-0-7627-7387-9

Printed in the United States of America

10 9 8 7 6 5 4 3 2 1

Restaurants and chefs often come and go, and menus are ever-changing.
We recommend you call ahead to obtain current information before
visiting any of the establishments in this book.

To Tim, who saw me through

CONTENTS

Acknowledgments

Though the primary focus of my career as a writer and teacher has been about home cooking, I am not a complete stranger to the world of restaurant kitchens. Like most writers I have had to do many other things to make those proverbial ends come closer to meeting, and have done my share of professional cooking as a caterer, restaurant cook, and personal chef in private homes. Contrary to popular belief, while there is a lot of satisfaction to be had from it, the life of a chef is not an easy one, and offers very little glamour. Those who choose that life have my deepest respect. My first thank you, then, must be to all of Savannah's professional cooks who have taken the time from their busy kitchens to share their craft and kitchen wisdom with me and help to bring this book to fruition.

A special thank you is due to friend and colleague Holly Herrick, who laid the groundwork for this book and did so much of the initial research before the project came into my hands, and was always ready to lend her help, advice, and sympathetic ear. So many people helped in small ways that they're too numerous to name, but I would be remiss if I did not particularly thank new friend Armide de la Gueronniere, who graciously helped with nothing more than a mutual friend to recommend me; old friend Bonnie Gaster, my link not only to the restaurants and cafes on her native Tybee Island, but to most of Savannah; and friend and colleague Tim Rutherford, who was always ready with advice, help, and key introductions. Thanks to everyone at Globe Pequot Press, particularly my editor, Katie Benoit Cardoso, and project editor Tracee Williams, for being ever kind, patient, and helpful no matter how cranky I got, and for encouraging me to keep going when I didn't think I could.

Perhaps the most important thank you of all is to the place that has been my home for these last thirty years, a place that still inspires me with its breathtaking beauty, embraces and warms me with its graciousness, and, of course, feeds me with its wonderfully unique cuisine.

Thank you, Savannah.

Introduction

The first thing to know about Savannah is that it is not a restaurant town.

Yes, there are many wonderful restaurants here—as the pages of this book attest—and for more than two centuries, the residents and visitors of this venerable port city have dined extremely well. There are even visitors who have come here especially to eat. Throughout Savannah's history, from the days of Tondee's Tavern in the unsettled time of the late colonial period and Revolution until the mid-twentieth century, there have always been a handful of memorable, even legendary public dining rooms—from the now-vanished Pulaski House Hotel and DeSoto Hotel to restaurants like Hester's Martinique and Johnny Harris to the cozy tearooms tucked into the cellar of the historic Andrew Low mansion (where the Girl Scouts of America was born) and a corner parlor of The Olde Pink House. However, Savannah has never been a city defined by its public tables in the same way that its sister cities Charleston and New Orleans have been. The city's truly refined cuisine, the sort that drew visitors and caused them to wax poetic in their letters and journals, was found mostly in private homes.

All of that is changing.

Today Savannah enjoys a lively and growing restaurant scene, from historic River Street along the city's namesake waterway to its suburban Southside and the easternmost marsh islands that form a buffer between the old city and the Atlantic Ocean. While this historic town will probably never be the kind of food destination spot that New Orleans and Charleston have become, it can certainly hold its own.

The End of an Era, the Start of a Revolution

One of the things that fueled modern Savannah's food culture was a cataclysmic occurrence that seems, on the surface, to have been a major culinary setback: the destruction of Savannah's historic food market on Ellis Square. Though considered by many to be an irreplaceable piece of the city's history, the handsome old building had been neglected and become run down and rather shabby. It was slated for destruction when a small band of preservationists rallied and launched a determined fight to save it. Their efforts were unhappily doomed to fail, and in 1955 the old City Market was reduced to rubble. In a misguided effort to keep shoppers downtown, it was replaced by a hulking parking garage that obliterated the square and did little to relieve the bourgeoning parking problem. Downtown Savannah would not see another successful open-air market until the launching of Forsyth Farmers' Market (see Market Fresh, page 101) more than half a century later.

But what seemed like a terrible setback was actually the catalyst that launched one of the largest and most successful preservation movements in American history—a movement that changed Savannah's future and, in an oblique way, ignited a new interest in dining well away from home. During the last half of the twentieth century, Savannah's historic downtown was refurbished and restored piece by piece. The signature charm that had always attracted visitors was revitalized, and tourism skyrocketed, infusing the sleepy downtown with renewed energy and, more to the point at hand, with visitors hungry for a taste of the region's legendary cooking. Places like Herb Traub's Pirate's House Restaurant in old Trustees' Garden and the Harris family's Shrimp Factory and River House Restaurants on River Street flourished. But as Savannah's reputation grew, so did its demand for more fine-dining opportunities.

Of the leaders in the ensuing movement that would change the face of Savannah's restaurant culture, three special people stand out: Chef Gerry Klaskala, his protégé Chef Walter Dasher, and the now legendary Chef Elizabeth Terry. In 1981, Chef Terry opened Elizabeth on 37th (see page 71), at first as a modest dessert cafe. Gradually the restaurant expanded to include lunch and dinner, and Chef Terry's elegant reinterpretations of traditional Lowcountry cookery, with its emphasis on fresh, local ingredients, soon gave the restaurant a regional and then national reputation. Winner of half a dozen awards, including the James Beard Foundation Award for best regional chef, Elizabeth Terry's restaurant became something of a culinary icon that has set a standard for generations of Savannah restaurateurs. Around the same time, Chef Klaskala rocked Savannah when he and business partner Sandy Hollander opened the legendary 45 South in, of all places, a Best Western motel on the Southside of town. With its starched linens, elegant old world decor, and cutting-edge cuisine, 45 South quickly became one

of the hottest restaurants in the region. After Klaskala moved on to shake up Atlanta with several award-winning restaurants and 45 South moved downtown to East Broad Street, Chef Walter Dasher kept the flame burning bright and added his own culinary genius to the mix. Though he has retired and the restaurant has since closed, their influence remains keen, since a number of young chefs who trained with Dasher in that kitchen have remained in Savannah and have led the city into a new culinary era.

None of this, of course, happened in a vacuum. Almost from its beginning, Savannah has been a food-loving city. The presently fashionable earth-to-table movement was actually a part of the city's original plan: The first residential lots not only contained a small kitchen garden but were also allotted a larger plot outside the city palisade for more serious gardening. And its picturesque squares, now carefully manicured parks, were originally intended for keeping livestock. For the first decade, imported provisions were basic, crude, and in short supply, but within a surprisingly short time, a distinct food culture began to emerge. By the early 1760s (a mere thirty years after its founding) the city's import merchants were offering a startlingly sophisticated assortment of goods, from the expected molasses, rum, sugar, flour, pickled meat, and potatoes to almonds, anchovies, capers, coffee, tea, olives, fresh and preserved gingerroot, and a wide assortment of cheeses that included English Cheddar, Cheshire, Gloucester, and Stilton, and, most likely, Italy's Parmigiano Reggiano—one of the world's earliest "traveling" cheeses. There were also copious quantities of Madeira and other fine wines available. By the beginning of the nineteenth century, when rice and cotton had made Savannah one of the wealthiest cities in the country, that food culture was well established. Wealthy Savannahians entertained lavishly at home and quickly gave Savannah an international reputation as "the Hostess City." But they also thought nothing of taking a boat to New York or Philadelphia for dinner and an opera, and most of them who took a Grand Tour spent more time eating their way through Europe than they did sightseeing.

But back to modern Savannah: The generations that have followed those culinary pioneers have taken the city's restaurant scene in an interesting and unexpected direction. While white-cloth restaurants like Elizabeth's, Alligator Soul, and Local 11Ten continue to flourish, there is a veritable explosion of small mom-and-pop cafes, diners, and take-out food shops that are owned and operated by classically trained chefs who have opted for a more casual way of sharing their craft. And even the chefs who have stayed the fine-dining course have changed the way they serve, making it possible for

their patrons to have everything from a simple, relatively inexpensive supper to a full five-course extravaganza.

There is also an exciting change in the way chefs of all walks acquire the provisions that fill their menus. Although local restaurants have always relied on the region's bountiful harvest of fish and shellfish from its sea and salt marshes, the farm land immediately surrounding Savannah had long since been developed into suburban neighborhoods and shopping malls. Until recently, fresh produce, meat, and dairy products were mostly trucked in from distant places. Today chefs are making a broader effort to stay local, reaching out to the growing number of regional farmers who are producing high-quality, organic, pasture-raised meat, vegetables, and dairy products. Regionally made cheeses and charcuterie are no longer a wishful notion, but a reality. The result is that the quality of the food from the neighborhood pizza, burger joint, and taqueria to the finest white-cloth dining room is better than ever.

My Savannah

This book has been quite an adventure and, I'll frankly own, not always an easy one. When I first came to Savannah thirty years ago, it was to practice architecture and preservation, not cooking. Dining options in those days were more limited, and we ate at home a lot. But cooking was in my blood, and before long, I began to teach cooking on the side, wrote a column about it for a local paper, and started my first cookbook. When I eventually left architecture altogether to make teaching and writing about cooking my full time vocation, I was still not what one would call a restaurant critic. Even now, my regular column for the *Savannah Morning News* is about home cooking.

Fortunately, when I did go out, I knew good cooking when I saw and tasted it, and luckily I made friends with Elizabeth Terry, Walter Dasher, and a few other professional cooks, friendships that I will always treasure. All the same, my world was—and until now has remained—that of the home cook. I came into this project midstream, taking it over from another writer. The restaurant choices had mostly been made, photographs had been taken, and it was up to me to bring it all together. Quite honestly, the waters were choppy. But happily, I have made many wonderful new friends, learned a lot, eaten very well indeed, and discovered a new dimension to cooking that has enriched the way I cook and eat—both at home and away from it. I used only to eat out for the rare celebratory splurge or when I was too tired to stand in front of the stove. It was, as one of my culinary teachers used to put it, all too often a blessing to eat at home after one of those outings. Now I often go out because I want to, and look forward to seeing what my culinary colleagues will be up to next.

I hope that this book will inspire you to do the same.

— Damon Lee Fowler
Savannah, October 2012

17Hundred90 Inn & Restaurant

307 East President Street
(912) 236-7122
www.17hundred90.com
Owner/General Manager: Patrick Godley
Co-Owner: Nathan Godley

The Historic District's Northeast Quadrant, bordered to the north by Bay Street, to the south by Oglethorpe Avenue, and to the west by Lincoln Street, is Savannah's oldest neighborhood, where you'll find the largest collection of Savannah's simple but elegant early architecture. It is also where you'll find one of the city's oldest—and by legend, most haunted—bed-and-breakfast inns: 17Hundred90. Named for the year that its main building is believed to have been built, this venerable inn is actually a collection of three Federal-style frame houses clustered around a central courtyard. Its elegant guest rooms and spooky reputation have long made it a favorite with visitors, but locals are drawn by its dining room.

Tucked into the raised basement (elegantly referred to by Savannahians as the "garden level"), its brick-paved floors, exposed brick walls, and time-darkened heart pine ceiling joists, warmed by working fireplaces, soft candlelight, and the opulent counterpoint of crystal chandeliers, lend the dining room the feel of another era, especially in cooler weather, when the fireplaces are blazing and candles glow in every window. Nightly live entertainment completes the mood, inviting guests to linger. The continental-style menu is not extensive, but changes seasonally, and its selections are thoughtfully chosen to feature local ingredients wherever possible

Tilapia Chesapeake

(SERVES 4)

At the Inn, Tilapia Chesapeake is offered in the spring, served over a simple risotto and garnished with asparagus and cherry tomatoes.

1¼ cups mayonnaise
Freshly squeezed juice of 1 lemon
¼ cup Worcestershire sauce
¼ cup heavy cream
2 tablespoons milk
2 large egg yolks
2 tablespoons Dijon mustard
1 tablespoon dry mustard powder
Old Bay Seasoning, to taste
Sweet paprika, to taste
4 (6-ounce) tilapia fillets
Lemon pepper, to taste
Olive or vegetable oil
1 cup lump crabmeat

Whisk together the mayonnaise, lemon juice, Worcestershire, cream, milk, egg yolks, and both mustards. Season to taste with Old Bay and paprika and set aside.

Lightly season the tilapia with Old Bay and lemon pepper. Prepare a grill and preheat it, and preheat the oven to 400°F. Brush the tilapia with oil and sear it on the grill until it is marked on both sides. Remove and put the fillets on an oiled baking dish or rimmed sheet pan. Top with fresh crabmeat and smother with the sauce. Bake for 4 to 6 minutes, or until the sauce is golden on top.

700 Drayton Restaurant

Mansion on Forsyth Park
700 Drayton Street
(912) 238-5158
www.mansiononforsythpark.com
Owners: The Kessler Collection

The steep terra-cotta-ornamented gables and slate-topped turrets of the Mansion on Forsyth Park, a luxury hotel overlooking Savannah's largest downtown park, make this sprawling Victorian-style building look settled and permanent, as if it has been around for at least a century. However, looks—especially in this old town—can be deceiving: While the core of the hotel, a slate-roofed brick and terra-cotta Romanesque Revival mansion, dates from 1889, most of the complex is brand new.

That original mansion, built by prominent architect Alfred S. Eichberg for Lewis Kayton and his family, is one of the key landmarks in this post–Civil War Victorian neighborhood. The southern end of Forsyth Park had been laid out as parade grounds for the military during the war, and those broad promenades and generous open lawns made the properties on its flanking avenues highly desirable. Not surprisingly, this is where Savannah's most opulent late Victorian and early twentieth-century homes were built, and its undisputed jewel was—and is—the Kayton mansion.

It is also one of the best preserved: When it had outlived its usefulness as a residence, unlike many of its neighbors, it was not cut up into apartments. Instead, its somber dark paneling and stained-glass windows made it an ideal setting for its next tenants, Fox and Weeks Funeral Home. For many years, the business was a downtown fixture, but after the funeral home relocated to the Southside, the mansion sat empty, and while most downtowners appreciated its value to the fabric of the Historic District, no one knew quite what to do with it. The future of the mansion was no longer secure. Fortunately, The Kessler Collection recognized its potential, and after removing modern additions that included an incongruous colonial-style chapel, they restored the house to its former opulence and used its architecture as inspiration for the design of the new hotel.

The original house is now the hotel's formal dining room and tavern, named 700 Drayton after its address. While its playfully modern decor nods back to the Victorian era, the cuisine is contemporary continental, and follows the trend toward fresh, seasonal, local ingredients. It has proved to be a popular dining spot not only for hotel guests but for locals as well. For guests bent toward a more hands-on experience, the Mansion's culinary program is not limited to the white-clothed elegance of its dining rooms. It also offers cooking classes in a fully equipped cooking studio, led by veteran cooking teacher Chef Darin Sehnert (see Kitchen Academics, page 50).

Al Salaam Deli

2311 Habersham Street (at 40th Street)
(912) 447-0400
Owner: Meqbel Salameh

When Jordan native Meqbel Salameh first came to the United States as a young man, he never imagined he'd end up finding a home in the Deep South. But a chance visit to a friend in Savannah put him in the path of the city's seductive charms, and before he knew it, he'd fallen in love with the place. In short order he also fell in love with his wife, Rose, a lovely, petite Savannahian who grew up on Tybee Island. The couple married, and he became a US citizen and eventually opened this tiny but irresistibly charming delicatessen. Today Meqbel and Rose spend their days side by side. She, with her head wrapped in a traditional hijab (she converted to Salameh's Muslim faith after their marriage), works at the counter, while he stays busy at the grill just a few steps away.

"Here, we do things differently," he explains of his diminutive deli's cozy family atmosphere. "When you love something, it makes a difference. My family, friends—we all eat here."

Salameh's only formal training was a long, successful stint as sous chef at a country club on nearby Hilton Head Island. He learned the art of cooking the old-fashioned way, from his mother and grandmother, first shopping for the best and freshest ingredients from the open-air markets of Jordan, and then cooking with them at home.

All the same, his menu at Al Salaam traverses the entire Mediterranean basin, taking its cues not only from Jordan but also Lebanon, Syria, Greece, and Egypt. Appropriately, *National Geographic* magazine covers literally paper the walls, and the air is perfumed with curry and garlic.

Calling himself a "student of humanity," Salameh is an ardent believer in the power that food, made with love, has to bring people together. His philosophy, both in the kitchen and in life in general, is simple: "Try your best to always do what's good and to do it from the heart."

Not surprisingly, he personally preps and cooks all the food, which has become a staple for scads (pardon the expression) of Savannah College of Art and Design (SCAD) students who stream through the place at all hours, drawn by Al Salaam's warm, homey atmosphere, delicious and comforting cooking, and student-friendly prices.

MEQBEL'S MARVELOUS BABA GHANOUSH

(SERVES 10–12 AS AN APPETIZER)

Salameh's version of baba ghanoush is a silky-rich, indulgent, and yet super-healthy roasted eggplant puree. Its subtle layers of flavor are brought to the fore and enhanced by a hint of smokiness that Salameh accomplishes by roasting the eggplant over an open gas flame or, when he can, on an outdoor grill. He sometimes varies the flavors by garnishing the puree with pomegranate seeds or chopped fresh mint.

4–5 medium-size eggplants

9 cloves garlic

3 cups tahini (sesame paste, available at Middle Eastern grocers and most supermarkets)

½ cup fresh-squeezed lemon juice

4 tablespoons white wine vinegar

¼ cup best-quality extra-virgin olive oil, plus additional for drizzling

Pinch of sea or kosher salt, to taste

Optional garnishes (use only one): 1 tablespoon finely chopped fresh parsley, 1 tablespoon pomegranate seeds, 1 tablespoon smashed mixture of fresh garlic and jalapeño pepper, or 1 tablespoon finely chopped fresh mint

Warm pita bread, cut into triangles, for serving

Position a rack in the center of the oven and preheat to 450° F.

Scrub the eggplants under cold water and pat dry. Put them on a rimmed baking sheet and roast until soft and concave, about 45 minutes. Alternatively, you may grill the eggplant over hardwood coals as Salameh often does: Position the rack about 8 to 10 inches from the coals and turn the eggplant frequently until the skin is evenly blistered and the flesh softened. Set aside until cool enough to handle, about 20 minutes.

In the bowl of a food processor or with a large mortar and pestle, crush the garlic to a smooth paste. Peel the eggplants and add the soft cooked flesh to the bowl of the food processor or mortar and pestle. Pulse or smash until smooth, silky, and aerated or work to a paste with the pestle.

Transfer the garlic/eggplant mixture to a large bowl, and whisk in the remaining ingredients. The texture should be light and smooth. Taste and adjust seasonings as needed. Turn the mixture out into a shallow dish and refrigerate until firmed and set, 30 to 60 minutes.

Serve in the one large dish or in several individual bowls, drizzled with more olive oil and sprinkled with the desired garnish. Serve with triangles of warm pita bread.

ALLIGATOR SOUL

114 BARNARD STREET (AT TELFAIR SQUARE)
(912) 232-7899
WWW.ALLIGATORSOUL.COM
OWNER/EXECUTIVE CHEF: CHRISTOPHER DINELLO
CO-OWNER: MAUREEN CRAIG

Take a few steps to the north of Telfair Square (one of the four originals and arguably one of the most historic), head down a short flight of stairs marked by an exuberant display of hanging flower baskets, and you'll find the cozy brick-vaulted cellar that's home to Alligator Soul. Founded in 2003 by the late Chef Hilary Craig and his wife, Maureen, this refined, continental-style restaurant is, by comparison to its historic neighborhood, a bit of a brash newcomer. But the timeworn brick vaults, exposed ceiling joists, and deep light-well windows of this circa-1885 space lend an Old World timelessness that make it seem to have been around forever. Moreover, Chef Craig's deft interpretations of classic Southern cooking, his insistence on making everything from the artisanal breads to the cured meats in-house, and his championship of the city's growing local food culture, quickly made Alligator Soul a fixture in downtown Savannah's fine dining scene.

Since Chef Craig's death in 2007, the kitchen has been presided over by Christopher DiNello, who came to Alligator Soul from The Union Square Cafe after he was handpicked by Craig to carry on his legacy. Chef DiNello became a partner in the restaurant in 2009, and, while he has respected Craig's original vision, he has made his own path.

"I've kept a few signature things of Hilary's," he says, but notes that over time he has put far more emphasis on local food products and traditions. He doesn't like to blindly order food he hasn't seen and touched—which means that most of his primary sources are local. "I like working with what I can physically touch before I bring it in to the kitchen. We're about 90 percent local now, but my goal is to eventually be a 100 percent."

"When you get things directly from the farmer," Chef DiNello points out, "you know where it came from, what's in it, and how fresh it really is. The freshest that the best supermarket farm-to-market program can offer is never less than two days from the field: That's not really fresh anymore. I like to get to know the farmers and work with the best that can be had from the area. I keep the preparation basic and clean—then introduce those one or two unexpected flavor components that get your attention."

Shrimp & Grits

(SERVES 4–6)

4 cups chicken stock or broth (or water)

1 cup heavy cream

¾ pound unsalted European-style butter

1 cup Georgia stone-ground grits

Salt and freshly milled black pepper

1 cup diced tasso ham

¼ cup freshly grated Parmigiano Reggiano,
    plus more for garnish (optional)

6 ounces grated mild to medium aged cheddar,
    plus more for garnish (optional)

2 tablespoons canola oil

2 tablespoons minced shallot or yellow onion

1–2 pounds large, fresh Georgia wild-caught shrimp,
    peeled and deveined

1 large or 2 medium cloves garlic, peeled and minced

¼ cup dry white wine

Creole spice blend, to taste

1 lemon wedge

¼ cup chopped flat-leaf parsley or cilantro

½ cup thinly sliced green onions

Put the chicken stock, cream, and 4 tablespoons butter in a heavy-bottomed saucepan and bring it to a simmer. Whisk in the grits and season with salt and pepper. Bring to a simmer, whisking constantly, and cook stirring often to avoid burning and sticking on the bottom, until it begins to thicken. Add the ham, stir well, and cook about 45 to 50 minutes, stirring often, until the grits are tender and thick. Stir in both cheeses and check the seasoning. The grits can be made a couple of days ahead; transfer them to a baking dish, cool, then cover and refrigerate until needed. To reheat, bring a small amount of stock or cream to a simmer in a saucepan and stir in the grits. Stir until soft and hot.

To prepare the shrimp: Heat a large sauté pan over medium-high heat. Add the oil and shallots and sweat briefly. Add the shrimp and sauté until they are almost cooked through, about 2 to 3 minutes, then add the minced garlic, toss until fragrant, and deglaze with the wine. Add a good pinch of Creole spice to taste, a splash of lemon juice, and the parsley or cilantro. Off the heat, swirl in the remaining butter until it is barely melted and the sauce is thick.

To serve: Divide the grits among four heated rimmed soup plates. Spoon the shrimp and butter sauce over them and sprinkle with the green onions and, if desired, a little more of the two cheeses.

Gallery Espresso

234 Bull Street (at Chippewa Square)
(912) 233-5348
www.galleryespresso.com

To fully appreciate Gallery Espresso, the bohemian-style coffeehouse that has overlooked Chippewa Square from the corner of Bull and Perry Streets for the last decade, it helps to know a little of where it began more than twenty years ago—just around the corner in the small half basement of an antebellum row house on Liberty Street. A few steps down from street level, its low ceiling was the exposed heart pine joists and boards of the floor above, and its walls were the rough Savannah gray brick of the building's foundation. Furnished with an eclectic mix of vintage cafe furniture and odd antiques, it was one of the few places in this tradition-bound city where avant-garde artists could show their work. It was not, however, the art on its walls that attracted regulars to this tiny basement coffeehouse, but the fact that it was for more than a decade just about the only place in downtown Savannah to get well-made espresso drinks, especially after regular business hours. Those were the early days of America's explosive love affair with espresso bars, and this little basement gallery quickly attracted a truly cross-cultural clientele of free-spirited art students, mature downtowners, and business professionals.

Eventually, Gallery Espresso outgrew the basement and spilled out onto the shaded sidewalk, but there soon came a time when even that could no longer accommodate the crowds. Moreover, Gallery was no longer the only game in around: National chains were beginning to find their way into downtown. Cramped and facing competition, the cafe pulled out its picture hooks and moved to its present home. Overlooking the historic square, with its ancient live oaks and imposing bronze statue of Savannah's founder, James Edward Oglethorpe, by celebrated American sculptor Daniel Chester French, this handsomely restored Victorian storefront offered a lot more than just a great view. It had double the space, lofty ceilings, and far better natural light for showing artwork. All that extra room, of course, meant more art and more eclectic furniture, which has made it feel more like a living room than coffeehouse. But that wasn't all that expanded: The coffee drinks are now supplemented by teas, old-fashioned fountain drinks (think Italian cream sodas and root-beer floats), and a modest wine list. It also offers a larger selection of food from breakfast pastries, to light salad and sandwich lunch fare, to locally made desserts. Gallery also sells signature coffee beans by the pound.

Angel's BBQ

21 West Oglethorpe Lane (Between Bull and Whitaker)
(912) 495-0902
www.angels-bbq.com
Owners: Andrew and Aileen Trice

Downtown pedestrians who find themselves on Bull Street on any weekday morning, whether they're an aimlessly strolling tourist or hustling destination-bound native, are often tempted off their path as they pass the imposing facade of Independent Presbyterian Church. It is not, however, the inspiring portico and soaring spire of this historic house of worship that tugs at them, but the beguiling aroma of hickory-wood smoke wafting down the lane next to it.

If they give in to temptation, that aroma will lead them to a neat, whitewashed-brick carriage house that, in its own modest way, is as historic as the elegant stone edifice next door. And if they're lucky, the black-painted carriage door will be open and a little yellow flag that simply reads BBQ will be fluttering in the breeze, the only sign that Angel's BBQ is open for business.

While the trim little historic building housing this iconic 'cue joint presents a conventional face to passersby, through its door one enters the wonderfully odd world of Chef Andrew Trice. The air is reassuringly perfumed with wood smoke, and the deli cooler setting off the tiny kitchen is covered with an array of barbecue sauces, all made in-house, that change with the season and Trice's experimental mood. The place is tiny, with only three tables, and the decor is what you might imagine if a retired pirate opened a roadside barbecue stand.

But this California Culinary Academy graduate is not, in fact, a retired pirate (though he looks a bit like one). Underneath his bright red chef's hat and mild, unassuming barbecue-pitmaster manner lurks the mind of a brilliant, quietly passionate cook. Wearied by the constant pressure for novelty and innovation in the fine-dining realm, he traded it in for a little barbecue joint that would give him the freedom to go his own way. And his barbecue does just that, defying classification. Though slow-cooked over hardwood until it practically melts off the bone, it's nothing like the traditional barbecue from this part of Georgia, but nor is it really Carolina, Memphis, or Kansas City style, either.

Angel's House Barbecue Sauce

(MAKES ABOUT 2 QUARTS)

The best way to experience the uniqueness of Chef Andi's barbecue is the Angel's Special, in which it is simply piled high on a sandwich bun, drizzled with house sauce, and topped with a generous helping of mustard-laced coleslaw. Here are the sauce and slaw that make the combination work. Note that, while it's pared down to a more manageable portion, the sauce recipe still makes a lot. Fortunately, it keeps for a very long time, and you'll find yourself using it for a lot more than just barbecued pork.

2 tablespoons (¼ stick) unsalted butter
1 cup cider vinegar
1 cup Worcestershire sauce
½ cup soy sauce
½ cup unsulfured molasses
3¼ cups tomato sauce
6 tablespoons yellow mustard
½ tablespoon hickory liquid smoke
3 cups water
3 ounces Mexican Coca-Cola (preferred) or Classic Coca-Cola

2 tablespoons Angel Dust Barbecue Rub (or your favorite)
2 generous dashes Tabasco Sauce

Combine all the ingredients in a heavy-bottomed pot and bring the mixture to a boil over medium heat. Lower the heat and simmer 5 minutes. Transfer to clean pint or quart canning jars; cool, cover, and refrigerate until needed.

Angel's Coleslaw

(SERVES 6–8)

The secrets to the coleslaw's bright flavor are mustard and kosher pickles.

3 cups mayonnaisc (Trice likes Duke's or Hellmann's)
3 cups prepared yellow mustard
⅔ cup honey
⅓ medium Vidalia onion, chopped fine
3 tablespoons chopped garlic
4–5 kosher dill pickle spears, chopped, to taste
Kosher pickle brine, to taste
Tabasco Sauce, to taste
2 pounds green cabbage, shredded
About ⅓ cup shredded red cabbage (optional)
About ⅓ cup shredded carrots

In a large mixing bowl, blend together the mayonnaise, mustard, honey, onion, garlic, and chopped pickle. Add a little of the pickle brine and a few dashes of Tabasco Sauce, both to taste.

Combine the cabbage, red cabbage (if using), and carrots in a separate bowl. Fold in the dressing until the slaw has the consistency that you like. Taste and adjust the pickle brine and Tabasco Sauce. Cover and refrigerate until needed, but for not less than 2 hours (to meld the flavors).

Angel's Peanut Collards

(SERVES 6–8)

While a lot of Southern barbecue joints serve collard greens, you aren't likely to find any like Andrew Trice's. Taking inspiration from west African cookery, in which greens with peanuts are classic, he adds peanut butter to bind the sauce at the end. He uses smooth peanut butter, but says you may use a chunky one if you want to add a little crunch.

2 pounds fresh collard greens

3 ounces (about 6 tablespoons) unsalted butter

2 tablespoons chopped garlic

2 tablespoons cider vinegar (plus or minus), to taste

3 tablespoons soy sauce

2 tablespoons Worcestershire sauce

12 ounces (about 1½ cups) chicken stock

4–6 dashes Tabasco Sauce, to taste

Black pepper, to taste

About 6 tablespoons peanut butter
  (Angel's uses smooth)

Remove the stems from the collard greens, stack several leaves together, cut them into ribbons, and then roughly chop them.

Put the butter, garlic, vinegar, soy sauce, Worcestershire, and stock into a large, heavy-bottomed pot.

Add the collards and several dashes of Tabasco Sauce, to taste. Cover and bring to a boil over medium heat, then cook, occasionally stirring them up from the bottom, until the greens are wilted.

Lower the heat and cook, stirring from time to time, until the greens are tender. Taste and adjust the vinegar and Tabasco, and add black pepper to taste.

Just before serving, stir in the peanut butter to bind the sauce, starting with 6 tablespoons, and adding more as needed. Let it heat through, turn off the heat, and serve at once.

Back in the Day Bakery

2403 Bull Street
(912) 495-9292
www.backinthedaybakery.com
Owners: Cheryl and Griffith Day

The Starland Dairy District, a commercial dairy complex on Bull Street, was at the heart of a thriving commercial district until mid-twentieth century, when the diary closed. Over the ensuing years, it fell on some pretty hard times, but since its renovation in the last decade, this once blighted area has again become a major player in Savannah's food scene. Within this three-block area, one can find everything from fresh lunch fare at The Starland Cafe (page 157), to fine European wines at Le Chai Galerie du Vin, to ribs and pulled pork from itinerant mom-and-pop barbecue vendors that set up in old service station lots on the weekends. The undisputed center of this culinary mecca is Back in the Day Bakery on the northeast corner of the old main dairy building.

The brainchild of Cheryl and Griffith Day, a bohemian couple who describe themselves as "home bakers who happen to own a little bake shop," this neighborhood bakery and cafe in only a few years has not only become a local icon but has established a reputation that is rapidly taking on national proportions. The name "Back in the Day" is more than just a play on its owners' surname; it's a direct description of the shop's character. Brightly decorated with Cheryl's collection of vintage kitchen toys and baking tools, its air redolent of baking bread, warm chocolate, buttercream, and espresso, and its hodgepodge of vintage tables and chairs lit by tall plate-glass windows on two sides of the building, the Days' establishment is, despite their modest assertion, no mere "little bake shop." It's the physical manifestation of their slogan, "Slow down and taste the sweet life."

That may sound like nothing more than a clever tag for selling cupcakes, but the Days mean it literally: They've committed to helping their customers slow the pace of their lives and, at least at the table, return to an easier time when good bread and pastries were meant to be leisurely savored. They're both deeply involved in the baking, taking equal responsibility for the shop's products. Cheryl, who grew up making cakes with her mother and grandmother, makes the pastries, cookies, and award-winning signature cupcakes. Griff, whose curiosity for the science of good bread making seems limitless, makes the rustic European-style breads that have earned the bakery a regular following well beyond Savannah's city limits, and keeps the seasonally changing lunch menu fresh and current.

From crusty, deeply satisfying baguettes and Pugliese-style loaves to the lavish two-person-size cinnamon buns (made only on Saturday), lavender-scented shortbread, and half a dozen varieties of cupcakes, the goods that fill Back in the Day's glass cases have a reassuringly homespun character that is not just like Mom's: They're the way you wish Mom had made them.

BAR · FOOD

4523 HABERSHAM STREET (HABERSHAM VILLAGE AT 42ND)
(912) 355-5956
WWW.BARFOODSAVANNAH.COM
OWNER/CHEF: JOHNNY BAKER
CO-OWNER: PAULA LETCHER

Take one part neighborhood pub, one part stylish Manhattan Asian-French fusion cafe, one part easy shorts-and-sandals comfort, throw in a dash of local sand-between-his-toes marsh rat (the nickname for locals who grew up on the barrier islands), shake it up in a brushed stainless cocktail shaker, and pour it into a frosty cocktail glass—and what you'll have is bar · food, a sleek little neighborhood cafe and bar in midtown's Habersham Village.

The brainchild of veteran chef and caterer Johnny Baker, this hopping little nightspot has a "place to be seen" decor and cutting-edge menu, but a laid-back everyone-knows-your-name attitude. Unlike other cafe-bar establishments, however, where the food is a forgettable afterthought, designed solely for speed of preparation and ease of serving, the menu offered here is thoughtfully designed to be tasty, memorable, and affordable, while pairing well with the bar's surprisingly wide selection of mixed drinks, wines, and bottled beers.

Baker is no stranger to the concept of the casual neighborhood tavern. Born and raised in Savannah's Isle of Hope community, this native son has been cooking for most of his life. After catering for years, in the late 1990s he opened his first restaurant, Queenie's, in a renovated service station a couple of miles to the north on this very same street.

Queenie's was sold in 2008 when Baker left Savannah to command the kitchen of a private yacht, but he was soon back home looking for a new location. He reconnected with former partner Paula Letcher, and together they found the ideal spot for their next venture in this food-centric midtown shopping enclave.

Hot Rice Bowl

(SERVES 4)

The menu is French-Asian fusion, and one of its quickest and most popular dishes is a Hot Rice Bowl, which as its name implies is simply a bowl of steaming long-grain rice topped with teriyaki sauce, kimchee, and a choice of pan-seared salmon, shrimp, chicken, duck, or ginger beef.

For the bar · food teriyaki sauce
(makes about 1¼ cups):

- 1 cup pineapple juice
- 1 tablespoon cornstarch
- 1 tablespoon soy sauce (more or less), to taste
- 1 teaspoon ground ginger
- 1 clove garlic, crushed and peeled
- ½ teaspoon ground white pepper or cayenne pepper

- About 2 tablespoons ginger oil (available at Asian grocers)
- 6 ounces center-cut salmon fillet
- 6 cups hot cooked long-grain Asian rice (such as jasmine; do not use converted rice)

- Kimchee (Korean/Southeast Asian cabbage pickle, available at Asian grocers)

Make the teriyaki sauce: Whisk together the pineapple juice and cornstarch in a small saucepan. Bring it to a simmer, stirring frequently, and simmer gently until thick. Whisk in the soy sauce, ginger, garlic, and pepper and let it simmer a few minutes longer to blend the flavors.

Film a well-seasoned or nonstick heavy-bottomed 11-inch skillet with ginger oil. Put the pan over medium-high heat, and when it is hot but not quite smoking, add the salmon fillet and sear well on both sides. Lower the heat and cook until it is done to your taste (in the cafe, Baker takes it up while still rare because it continues to cook sitting on the hot rice). Remove it from the heat.

Divide the rice into individual Asian noodle bowls or deep cereal bowls, allowing 1½ cups per serving. Top with the salmon and drizzle with teriyaki sauce to taste. Serve with additional sauce and kimchee passed separately.

HABERSHAM VILLAGE

The heart of Savannah's midtown, a suburban neighborhood that sprouted in the 1950s on what was then the southern edge of town, is Habersham Village, a neat, compact shopping center of the same vintage. Clustered in a three-block area on either side of Habersham Street, this shopping district, unlike many other urban strip centers of the era, has the look and feel of a village Main Street. There are all the usual neighborhood essentials—a bakery, grocery, drugstore, package store, florist, and service station, just to name a few. There's also a pet store and popular children's clothing emporium. One would little suspect that it was also a destination for local food lovers. Between Habersham Beverage Warehouse at the southern tip, one of Savannah's largest wine dealers, and Bella's Italian Cafe (page 24) at its extreme

northern end, there are half a dozen cafes and food-related businesses, including bar · food (page 18), Ogeechee River Coffee Roasters (see Local Roasted, page 118), a burrito joint, a neighborhood diner, and a sushi bar.

The grocery, Jones Red & White Market, is the kind of mom-and-pop neighborhood grocery rarely seen anymore, and it is, in a way, a microcosm of the entire village. While it offers the usual groceries found in any small supermarket, it has uniquely tailored itself for its neighborhood, which is an unusual blending of born-and-bred Southerners of all races, upscale urban professionals who have come from larger cities, and an international assortment of college students. In what other grocery would patrons be met at the door by the appetite-stirring aroma of hickory wood smoke? Instead of the usual deli, Jones Market has a barbecue joint located at the back of its produce department, offering up ribs, pulled pork, and chickens roasted over hardwood. This is also where Savannahians from other parts of town come to shop for fresh, local produce. Where else would you find Georgia peaches, Silver Queen corn, fresh collards, turnip greens, field peas, and green peanuts for boiling right alongside arugula, shiitake mushrooms, and serrano chile peppers? You'll also find imported brie and Roquefort in the dairy case and smoked ham hocks and pigs' ears in the meat cooler. And, of course, there is a selection of national brands of specialty ice cream in the freezer section and specialty cookies in the snack aisle. It all adds up to a unique shopping experience that keeps the traffic on this stretch of Habersham Street lively and the diagonal parking that lines either side of it filled with cars from all over town.

BELFORD'S SEAFOOD AND STEAKS

315 WEST ST. JULIAN STREET
(912) 233-2626
WWW.BELFORDSSAVANNAH.COM
OWNER: KEVIN MCPHERSON

One of the key anchors of downtown's thriving City Market District (see pages xv and 66) is the Belford Building at the corner of St. Julian and Montgomery, just across from newly restored Franklin Square. Believed to have been designed by Hyman W. Witcover, a local architect who was responsible for, among many other downtown monuments, Savannah's imposing domed City Hall, it was completed in 1902 for Savannah's Hebrew congregation. It sold a decade later to grocery wholesaler W. T. Belford (whose weathered sign can still be seen on the west side of the building) and has been known as the Belford Building ever since. The deep sidewalk facing St. Julian, lofty ceilings, warm, exposed brick walls, and tall, arched transom-topped windows and doors facing both St. Julian and Congress Streets all make this an ideal home for a fine-dining restaurant such as Belford's Seafood and Steaks.

Because St. Julian Street has been restricted to pedestrian traffic, the sidewalk on the north side of the building has become an inviting outdoor cafe. Shaded by a deep awning and cooled by lazily spinning paddle fans, it stays full at both lunch and dinner on all but the coldest of days. Inside, the airy, sunlit dining room is a popular lunch spot for businessmen, local shoppers, and tourists alike, and it provides an ideal setting for one of downtown's most popular Sunday Champagne brunches. This is not just a daytime venue, however: Live entertainment and warm, soft lighting also make it an equally popular evening destination.

BELFORD'S SHE-CRAB SOUP

(SERVES 6–8)

Though its real specialty is fresh local seafood, Belford's is also known for its grilled prime steaks, and it offers a small but thoughtful selection of pasta and risotto. A signature appetizer is a thick, rich crab soup that is Belford's take on a Lowcountry classic. She-crab soup is so called because it is delicately colored and flavored with the bright, coral-colored roe of a female blue crab. Since overharvesting of female crabs has led to regional restrictions, however, many Lowcountry cooks have found ways of using things other than roe to flavor the soup. The cooks at Belford's use a combination of finely diced red bell pepper and tomato paste to give the soup the characteristic coral-pink hue and a subtly sweet flavor.

½ pound (2 sticks) unsalted butter
¼ cup finely diced onion
¼ cup finely diced carrots
¼ cup finely diced red bell peppers
¼ cup finely diced celery
½ cup flour
1 cup crab or seafood stock
4 cups heavy cream
4 cups half-and-half
½ cup dry sherry
1 tablespoon tomato paste
1 pound crab claw meat, picked through for shell

In a heavy-bottomed pot, slowly melt the butter over medium-low heat. When the butter is melted, add the onions, carrots, bell peppers, and celery and cook until the onions are clear. Slowly whisk in the flour to make a fairly thick roux. Lower the heat and cook for about 15 to 20 minutes, but don't allow the roux to brown.

Increase the heat to medium and whisk in the crab stock and allow it to thicken, whisking constantly. Slowly whisk in the cream and simmer, whisking, until it has thickened as well.

Finally, whisk in the half-and-half, let it thicken, and then reduce the heat to a bare simmer. Let it simmer for at least 1 hour, never allowing it to come to a boil, since it will scorch easily. Just before removing it from the heat, whisk in the sherry, tomato paste, and crabmeat.

Let it heat to 165°F, and remove it from the heat and serve.

Bella's Italian Cafe

4420 Habersham Street (at 41st Street)
(912) 354-4005
WWW.BELLASCAFE.COM
Owners: Joyce and Jim Shanks

Nestled in a corner in the north end of Habersham Village, a shopping hub in Savannah's midtown, you'll find Bella's Italian Cafe, a neighborhood bistro of the sort that every community dreams of having as its centerpiece. It's one of those cozy, family-run cafes in the style of an Italian trattoria, where the food is simple but delicious and soul satisfying, and the owners, in this case veteran restaurateurs Joyce and Jim Shanks, know not only their customers but each customer's favorites as well.

Since Bella's opened in 1993, an entire generation has been weaned on their spaghetti and meatballs, grown up on the pizza and manicotti, gotten engaged over the baked ziti with sausage, and are now bringing up their own children to share in the tradition.

Bella's is named for Joyce Shank's grandmother Bella Sorbilli, a diminutive woman born in Naples whose passion for cooking was as large as she was small. She and her husband, William, were considered among the best cooks in their Brooklyn neighborhood, and were legendary for their pasta fagiola (pasta and bean soup), baked manicotti, lasagna, and marinara. Grandma Bella's kitchen, like her heavily accented speaking voice, never strayed very far from her Italian roots, and it's the memory of her cooking that inspired many of the dishes on the cafe's menu.

BELLA'S MANICOTTI

(SERVES 6)

One of the most popular of the cafe's dishes is the manicotti, which Joyce has tried to get as close to her grandmother's as possible. A simple mélange of creamy ricotta-filled tubes of pasta and house-made marinara, it encapsulates the spirit and charm both of the woman who created it and the cafe that is her namesake.

For Bella's marinara (makes 6 cups):

2 (28-ounce) cans whole San Marzano tomatoes
    with juice
¼ cup extra-virgin olive oil
1 large yellow onion, peeled and diced
4 cloves garlic, peeled and chopped
½ medium carrot, peeled and chopped
¼ cup chopped thyme
1 fresh or dried bay leaf
1 teaspoon kosher salt

For the manicotti:

12 manicotti tubes (about 1 [1-pound] box; Bella's
    uses Barilla)
1 (15-ounce) container whole milk ricotta
½ pound fontina cheese, coarsely grated
2 cups freshly grated Parmigiano Reggiano
1 pound whole milk mozzarella, grated

Make the marinara: Crush the tomatoes by hand. They can be as finely crushed or as chunky as you like. Set them aside with their juices. Put the oil into a large, heavy-bottomed pot (preferably stainless steel lined) over medium heat. Add the onion, garlic, and carrot and sauté until the onions are transparent but not browned, about 10 minutes.

Add the thyme and bay leaf and cook, stirring, 5 minutes longer. Add the tomatoes with their juice and the salt. Stir well and cook at a gentle simmer for 30 minutes, stirring occasionally from the bottom, and adjusting the heat as necessary to keep it from scorching. This can be made several days ahead; cool and refrigerate in a well-covered glass jar or bowl.

Cook the manicotti according to the package directions to slightly more firm than al dente. Drain and set aside. Preheat the oven to 400°F.

Make the cheese filling: Blend together the ricotta, fontina, and 1 cup Parmigiano. In a separate bowl, mix together the remaining Parmigiano and mozzarella and set it aside.

To finish: Rub a 9 x 13-inch baking dish with olive oil and spread 3 cups marinara over the bottom. Stuff each manicotti tube with about ¼ cup cheese filling, making sure the filling completely extends to both ends of the tube. You may split the tubes lengthwise, spoon in the filling, and fold it back over to wrap the filling. Arrange them as they are completed on the prepared dish. Evenly cover the manicotti with the remaining 3 cups sauce and spread the mozzarella/Parmigiano mixture evenly over the top.

Cover with aluminum foil and bake 30 minutes. If a browned top is desired, remove the foil for the last 5 minutes or so of cooking. Let rest a few minutes before serving.

Johnnie Ganem's

Package and Wine Shop
501 Habersham Street (at Gaston Street)
(912) 233-3032
www.johnnieganem.com
Owners: Louise Ganem and Family

The now legendary tale that is told of Savannah, Charleston, and Augusta is that the question asked by residents of these Lowcountry sister cities when sizing up a newcomer actually gives away more about the character of the town than they want you to know. In Charleston, they ask "who your people are," in Augusta, "what your church is," and in Savannah, "what your drink is." There's another one that goes something like this: "Wherever two or three Savannahians are gathered, there's always a 'fifth.'" It should be no surprise, then, that the town forum is the local package store. And since 1942, that forum for downtowners has been Johnnie Ganem's. Even Baptists meet here—and speak to one another. Beginning as a small package store on the corner of Price and Gaston, it moved a block west to its present location in 1949. Family owned, with three generations actively involved (Johnnie's widow, Louise, still comes in to work every day, and her granddaughter recently joined the staff), this has never been just a liquor store: It was also a lounge, soda fountain, and popular curbside lunch spot.

By the mid-1950s, the food-service side of the business was doing so well that Johnnie and Louise opened Habersham House restaurant and eventually expanded to include the building next door, whose downstairs became the Steak Ranch, famed for its signature Garbage Steak (a 12-ounce tenderloin that Johnnie firmly believed had to be served the day it was cut or it was garbage, hence the name), and upstairs became the Rebel Ballroom, a popular dining and dancing spot. The restaurant closed in 1981, but the tradition for fine food at Ganem's continues with a full-service delicatessen and catering service, run by Johnnie and Louise's son, Chef Paul Ganem, whose cooking has become a legend in its own right.

Whether they are picking up that necessary fifth for a cocktail party, looking for the perfect wine to pair with dinner, or ordering a bottle of fine vintage Madeira, a wine that Savannah almost single-handedly made into a legend, downtowners know that Ganem's is the place not only to get it, but to get the best advice on selecting, storing, and serving it, not to mention a great deli platter to go with it—and, in the way of all good forums, the latest gossip.

Blowin' Smoke BBQ

514 Martin Luther King Jr. Boulevard
(912) 231-2385
www.blowinsmokebbq.com
Owners: Brian and Jennifer Huskey
Executive Chef: Jeffrey Crumpton

One of the last pockets of Savannah's historic downtown to enjoy widespread revitalization is the old West Broad Street corridor, now renamed in honor of slain civil rights leader Dr. Martin Luther King Jr. Traditionally "Main Street" to Savannah's African-American community, its south end had fallen on hard times after desegregation. Fortunately, all that has changed, and today this boulevard is one of downtown's most up-and-coming dining and shopping hubs. At its heart in more ways than one is Brian and Jennifer Huskey's Blowin' Smoke BBQ. One part Deep South barbecue joint and one part blues club, this neighborhood bistro's clientele runs the full gamut of Savannah's downtown population—from art students, to young families with strollers, to settled older couples and tourists.

The Huskeys are an energetic, enterprising young couple who also own B. Matthews (see Breakfasting Downtown at the Corner Cafe, page 128), an upscale neighborhood cafe on Bay Street, Blue Turtle Bistro, a sunny, beachy midtown cafe, and, as if that wasn't enough for them to do, Abe's on Lincoln, an old-fashioned tavern just a block from Reynolds Square.

The idea for Blowin' Smoke was planted, oddly enough, at their first Thanksgiving dinner in Savannah. Just three months after they bought B. Matthews Eatery on East Bay Street, Brian and Jennifer hosted more than twenty people for the holiday meal in the restaurant. Jeff Crumpton, an old high school friend of Brian's, smoked several racks of ribs for the dinner and slathered them with his own unique sauce. After only one bite of that sauce, Brian says he thought, "If we ever open a barbecue place, Jeff will be the one to do it."

Crumpton did try to talk them into shifting B. Matthews toward barbecue, but it already had an established following that they didn't want to change. They did, however, stay open to the idea, and when this handsomely restored building on MLK became available, with its spacious, high-ceilinged dining room, large side patio, and fully equipped kitchen, they decided to take the plunge—with, of course, their rib-smoking friend at the helm of the kitchen.

BLOWIN' SMOKE FRIED PICKLES
WITH SMOKY RANCH DRESSING

(SERVES 8–16)

A specialty of the house (aside from Crumpton's signature ribs and sauce) is fried pickles, which are offered as both appetizer and side dish. Fried pickles, usually dill sandwich chips coated with cornmeal batter, have been a fixture at Southern fish camps and barbecue joints since the '80s, but Blowin' Smoke ups the ante by rolling whole kosher spears in Parmesan cheese and cracker meal and offers ranch dressing blushed with barbecue sauce for dipping. They're dangerously addictive: One bite through the cracking, crisp crust to the sour, garlicky bite of the warm but still crunchy pickle inside, and you'll be hooked.

1 cup ranch-style dressing

3 tablespoons Kansas City–style barbecue sauce (Blowin' Smoke uses their own)

4 cups all-purpose flour

Salt, to taste

4 cups fine cracker meal (or dry bread crumbs)

⅓ cup lemon-pepper seasoning (available in any supermarket)

1¼ cups freshly grated Parmesan cheese

4 cups buttermilk

½ cup hot sauce (Texas Pete preferred)

Canola or vegetable oil, for deep frying

16 deli-style garlic dill pickle spears

In a mixing bowl, combine the dressing and barbecue sauce, cover, and refrigerate until needed.

Put the flour in a wide, shallow bowl and mix it with salt to taste. In another bowl, combine the cracker meal, lemon pepper, and Parmesan. In a third bowl, stir together the buttermilk and hot sauce.

Put enough oil into a deep fryer or deep, heavy-bottomed pot to come no more than halfway up the sides and heat it to 325°F. Dry the pickles on paper towels and roll them in the flour. Shake off the excess and dip them in the seasoned buttermilk. Lift them out, letting the excess flow back into the bowl, and then roll them in the cracker meal.

Slip the pickles, a few at a time, into the hot fat and fry until golden brown, about 5 minutes. Blot on absorbent paper and serve hot with smoky ranch dressing on the side.

Brasserie 529

529 East Liberty Street
(912) 238-0045
www.brasserie529.com
Owners: Amber and Chef John Roelle

Nestled among lush beds of herbs and flowering shrubs, the white cloths of its patio tables dappled by the shade of ancient live oaks, Brasserie 529 looks a bit like something Renoir might have painted had he ever come to Savannah. And that's exactly what Chef John Roelle and his wife, Amber, set out to create—a classic brasserie in the style of the Belle Époque that still feels at home in Savannah. Originally, brasseries were simply neighborhood taverns that served locally brewed beer and wine and hearty, simple food—pretty much the French version of a village pub. Chef Roelle first experienced such places when he lived in Poland during his high school years. But it was only after he went to France and saw the original brasseries, with their mosaic tile floors, yards of mirrors and polished brass, bentwood chairs and banquettes, and crisp, white-clothed tables, that he fell in love with the concept.

"This was long before I had any idea that I'd ever do anything like this," he explains, motioning toward Brasserie's casually opulent dining room.

Roelle, a Johnson & Wales graduate who trained with James Burns at New York's iconic Tavern on the Green, discovered Savannah while working in Charleston, and fell in love with its Old World atmosphere and laid-back pace. When he decided it was time to venture out and open his own place, he knew exactly what he wanted to do: move to Savannah and create a classic brasserie like the ones he had loved in France, a true neighborhood hub, one that looked back to the heyday of the Belle Époque brasseries but also reflected Savannah's casually elegant style. He has succeeded: With its walls of gilt-edged mirrors, vintage clock hanging over the bar, tufted banquettes, polished sconces, and shady dining patio, Brasserie successfully pays homage to its French namesakes, but has a relaxed elegance in tune with its historic neighborhood.

The menu is likewise a faithful nod to French brasserie fare—simple, hearty, yet elegant classics done right rather than "reinvented"—satisfying onion soup gratinéed with a light blanket of golden gruyère, roasted marrow accented with caviar, steamed mussels perfumed with Pernod, steak with pommes frites. There is also a selection of daily changing, freshly baked artisanal French breads made in house. Yet, despite its solidly French theme, the cuisine makes a more than passing nod to Savannah traditions, and Roelle relies heavily on ingredients from local farmers, fishermen, and ranchers for his seasonally changing menu.

Marrow & Caviar

(SERVES 4)

Roasted marrow is a much underappreciated delicacy today, but it was once relished by the denizens of nineteenth-century brasseries. Roelle has brought it back, adding a touch of luxury with a spoonful of caviar.

4 canoe-cut veal marrow bones (see note below)
Oil
4 tablespoons sturgeon caviar
Mixed micro greens such as baby cress, arugula,
    or frisée (not "spring mix")

Preheat the oven to 425°F. Put the marrow bones cut side up in a roasting pan or rimmed baking sheet. Brush lightly with oil and roast until browned, about 30 minutes. Let stand 2 to 3 minutes. Transfer to serving plates, cut side up, and top one end with a tablespoonful of caviar. Garnish the plate with greens and serve immediately.

Note: A canoe cut is a marrow bone (usually of veal) that is sawn lengthwise in half. Roelle gets them from Hunter Cattle Company (see sidebar, page 85). They're available only from specialty food vendors and by special order from a few butchers.

Moules 529

(SERVES 2)

Roelle takes steamed mussels, another brasserie standard, perfumes them with Pernod, and mixes in a selection of seasonal vegetables. They're offered two ways—alone as a first course, or with a basket of crisp pommes frites as a hearty main dish. At the Brasserie, they're made to order in single servings, but they can be made in two-serving batches, as given here. If you want more, just make additional batches as needed. Roelle says, "Once you get that pan heated up, you can make one right after the other."

2½ pounds mussels

1 tablespoon minced garlic

½ cup minced shallots

About 2 cups of an assortment of seasonal vegetables such as *haricots verts,* grape tomatoes, julienned sweet peppers

About 6 tablespoons dry white wine

About 6 tablespoons Pernod

About 1 cup fish stock

1 crusty baguette, for serving

Scrub and trim the "beard" from the mussels and set aside. Preheat a deep, heavy-bottomed pan over medium-high heat until it is almost smoking hot. Add the garlic, shallots, and mussels and toss until the mussels begin to open a little. Add the vegetables and keep tossing until they just begin to soften.

Deglaze the pan with the wine and Pernod, then add the fish stock. Bring it to a boil and cook, stirring or shaking the pan to redistribute the mussels, until they are fully opened. Ladle into large shallow bowls and serve at once with bread.

Butterhead Greens Café

1813 Bull Street
(912) 201-1808
www.butterheadgreens.com
Chefs/Owners: Patrick Zimmerman and Seth Musler

On the shady corner of Brady and Bull Street, just across from the stately 1920s Georgian Revival Richard Arnold High School (now SCAD's Arnold Hall), stands a little green-and-black painted Victorian storefront, the home of Butterhead Greens Café. With the atmosphere of a neighborhood mom-and-pop grocery enlivened by a bohemian artist's pad decor, this small but lively take-out spot mainly caters to the college students across the way. However, its friendly, youthful staff and student-budget-friendly menu of fresh-from-scratch sandwiches, salads, soups, and house-made flavored waters and teas have found a following among a much broader clientele from the area's other businesses and professional offices.

One of the reasons for such a diverse customer base is that Butterhead Green's classically trained chefs/owners, Patrick Zimmerman and Seth Musler, take their sandwiches, soups, and salads as seriously as they would an entree in a four-star restaurant. Both are ardent champions of seasonal cooking with fresh local ingredients, and they like to support local farmers and businesses as much as possible. For example, their freshly ground house-blend coffee is provided by local roaster Perc Coffee (see Local Roasted, page 118), a business just a few blocks south of the cafe.

The flavors are simple but layered, and include elements not normally associated with a take-out sandwich shop—sherry vinegar, extra-virgin olive oil, truffle oil, and fresh herbs. Standing on the counter by the register is a tall glass urn filled with daily-changing flavored water enhanced by unusual combinations of fruit, vegetables, and herbs—strawberry-basil, cucumber-mint, orange-cilantro. Spicy house-made cucumber and onion pickles enliven the salads and sandwiches.

Butterhead Greens Pickled Onions

(MAKES ABOUT 8 CUPS)

This simple pickle is terrific on pork, chicken, or tuna sandwiches, and gives a nice lift to mixed green and potato salads. Note that it must marinate for at least a day before the pickles will be ready to eat.

4 medium red onions, trimmed, halved, peeled, and sliced very thin
1 bay leaf
½ tablespoon whole peppercorns
3 tablespoons white sugar
3 tablespoons brown sugar
⅓ cup kosher salt
1 tablespoon dried thyme
2 cups cider vinegar
2 cups water

Special Equipment: **cheesecloth, twine**

Put the onions in a large nonreactive, heatproof glass or stainless-steel container. Combine the bay leaf, peppercorns, sugars, salt, thyme, vinegar, and water in a stainless-steel or enamel-lined pot and it bring to a boil over medium-high heat. Pour this through a strainer over the onions, reserving the solids.

Wrap the reserved solids in a double layer of cheesecloth and tie securely with twine to make the sachet. Add this to the onions and pickling liquid and weight down the onions with a plate to keep them submerged. Let stand at room temperature for 24 hours, then refrigerate and enjoy.

Butterhead Greens Sweet Potato Salad

(SERVES 6–8)

One of the most popular sides at Butterhead Greens is an unusual sweet potato salad dressed with honey, sherry vinegar, and olive oil and studded with chopped red onions and toasted pecans. Serve it with chicken or pork.

3 pounds sweet potatoes, peeled and cut into ½-inch cubes
1 small red onion, diced small
⅓ cup honey
⅓ cup sherry vinegar
2 tablespoons minced fresh thyme
⅓ cup chopped and toasted pecans
2 tablespoons extra-virgin olive oil
Salt and freshly milled black pepper, to taste

Put the sweet potatoes in a large, heavy-bottomed pot and cover them with water. Bring them to a boil, reduce the heat, and simmer until the potatoes are cooked through but still firm, 5 to 10 minutes, depending on the potatoes.

Drain the potatoes and add the onion, honey, vinegar, thyme, pecans, and olive oil. Gently toss to mix, season to taste with salt and pepper, then gently toss again and let cool. Serve at room temperature or chilled.

CAFE 37

205 EAST 37TH STREET
(912) 236-8533
WWW.CAFE37.COM
CHEF/OWNER: BLAKE ELSINGHORST

On the corner of 37th and Abercorn Streets, just a block east of the famed Elizabeth on 37th (see page 71), is a rambling Arts and Crafts mansion that today houses a busy antiques-and-design emporium. Tucked behind it, in a white-trimmed yellow carriage house, is one of Savannah's great gastronomical secrets—a charming little bistro simply called Cafe 37.

Looking as if it has been plucked right out of the south of France, this serene little spot is the domain of Blake Elsinghorst, a dynamic and forward-looking young chef who preaches a gospel of fresh, local ingredients; clean, precise flavors; and simple preparation.

Surprisingly, Chef Elsinghorst first came to Savannah not to cook, but to study graphic design and art history at the Savannah College of Art and Design (see page 146). As he worked his way through school in the area's best restaurants, however, he soon fell hard for the energy of a commercial kitchen, and decided he'd rather spend his life cooking than sitting at a computer. After he finished school, he pulled up roots, moved to Paris, and enrolled in Le Cordon Bleu, where he took a double course of study. He stayed on in France for another year after that, working for the likes of Chef Guy Martin, who he says is one of the most brilliant and innovative chefs in that country, and a big influence on his own cooking style.

After returning to the States, he landed briefly in New York, then eventually found his way back to Savannah, where he worked once again in some of the area's top restaurants. When he decided it was time to venture out on his own, he didn't have to look far to find the right place to do it; in a way, the right place found him.

"I just happened to drive by here one day and took one look and said, 'That's it! That's my restaurant!' I mean, just look at it," he points at the trim little carriage house. "Doesn't it look as if it was meant to be a restaurant?"

The thing he loves best is that the dining room is on the garden level, so the kitchen is upstairs, with windows all round it. "Most restaurant kitchens are in the basement or a room with almost no windows—lit by all these fluorescent lights. It's insane!"

Perhaps that airy, tree-house-like kitchen is one reason that the cooking, which Chef Elsinghorst describes as "local ingredients treated with a European sensibility" is so bright and innovative, yet unpretentious. The cafe is open for lunch daily but for dinner only on Thursday through Saturday evenings, so it specializes in small, simple plates such as this composed salad.

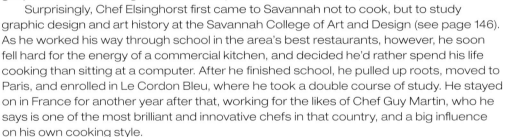

Salade au Roquefort

ROASTED PEAR & ROQUEFORT SALAD
WITH GRILLED CHICKEN & BUTTERMILK DRESSING

(SERVES 4)

With its warm roasted pear and Roquefort cheese contrasted with cool greens in buttermilk dressing and finished with crisp candied walnuts and grilled chicken, this is one of Cafe 37's most popular offerings.

4 organic, free-range boneless, skinless chicken breasts

Salt and freshly milled black pepper

2 tablespoons butter or canola oil

2 Anjou pears

1 tablespoon canola oil

4 ounces Roquefort cheese, crumbled

For the buttermilk dressing (makes about 3 cups):

2 cups nonfat buttermilk

1 clove garlic, crushed and peeled

1 teaspoon xanthan gum (available at specialty grocers and some supermarkets)

1 cup canola oil

1 pound spring mix

1 cup candied walnuts (available at specialty grocers) or plain walnuts

Preheat the oven to 325°F. Wipe the chicken dry and season with salt and pepper. Heat the butter in a sauté pan or skillet over medium heat, add the chicken, and sauté until cooked through, about 8 to 10 minutes, depending on thickness. Let rest a few minutes, then chop into bite-size pieces.

Halve the pears and remove the core with a melon baller. Film an ovenproof, nonstick pan with the oil and warm it over medium heat. Put in the pears, cut side down, and cook until lightly caramelized. Turn the pears cut side up and stuff the cavities with a rounded tablespoon of Roquefort per pear. Bake until the cheese is melted.

Make the buttermilk dressing: Put the buttermilk, garlic, and xanthan gum in the jar of a blender, cover, and blend for 1 minute. With the motor running, slowly add the oil until thickened. Refrigerate until needed and reshake before serving.

To plate: Toss the greens with just enough of the buttermilk dressing to lightly coat them. Divide them among four individual serving plates and top with the chicken, walnuts, and roasted pear. Serve immediately.

CHA BELLA

102 EAST BROAD STREET
(912) 790-7888
WWW.CHA-BELLA.COM
GENERAL MANAGER: MICHAEL LACY
EXECUTIVE CHEF: AMIE LINTON

For decades, tourists by the hundreds have flocked to Savannah's Trustees' Garden on East Broad Street, drawn by The Pirates' House, an eccentric themed restaurant inspired by a reference to Savannah in Robert Louis Stevenson's *Treasure Island.* But for the last few years, visitors have been discovering another reason to visit this shady, divided avenue, one that locals have known about for a long time: a charming bistro called Cha Bella.

In a town that prides itself on its eccentricities, perhaps nothing is more eccentric than this iconic neighborhood cafe with an Italian-sounding name, outdoor dining pavilion furnished with upholstered furniture, and extensive backyard kitchen garden. Add a group of energetic young owners who come from all over the map, and you have a real

cross-section of Savannah's quirky, cosmopolitan downtown community.

Actually, the name "Cha Bella" has nothing to do with Italy, but was coined from the names of its original owner's children. And while succeeding owners have taken advantage of its Italian sound, this has never been an Italian restaurant. Executive chef Amie Linton explains, "We are not Italian: We're American organic cuisine."

Nevertheless, they, too, have taken advantage of the Italian overtones by featuring seasonally changing risotti and house-made gnocchi and pasta. The real emphasis, however, is on fresh, local (and whenever possible, organic) ingredients—which brings us to that garden in the backyard. Conceived by former executive chef Matt Roher, it does a lot more than provide fresh herbs and produce for the kitchen; it represents a commitment to bring Cha Bella's patrons back to an intimate relationship with the land that extends well beyond that backyard plot. The seasonally changing menu also features freshly harvested local seafood and regional products.

Sautéed Georgia Shrimp with
Carolina Gold Risotto & Seasonal Vegetables

(SERVES 4)

Nothing better illustrates Chef Bhousle's philosophy than Cha Bella's risotti. Instead of the fat, medium-grained rice traditionally used for this dish, they're made with locally grown Carolina Gold, a delicately nutty long-grain rice that once made the Carolina and Georgia Lowcountry wealthy. Here it's topped with local Georgia white shrimp (a shellfish found in the deep waters just off the coast from Savannah) and a seasonal selection of vegetables.

For the risotto:

2 tablespoons olive oil

1 medium yellow onion, chopped

1½ cups Carolina Gold rice (or use arborio)

1 bay leaf

1 cup dry white wine

About 4 cups hot vegetable stock

¾ cup freshly grated Parmigiano Reggiano

2 tablespoons unsalted butter

Salt and whole black pepper in a mill

For the sautéed shrimp in white wine and tarragon
   sauce:

¼ cup olive oil

1 tablespoon minced garlic

24–28 large Georgia white shrimp, peeled and deveined

1 cup cherry or grape tomatoes, halved

1 cup fresh asparagus, trimmed and cut into
   2- to 3-inch lengths

½ cup dry white wine

Lemon juice, to taste

1 tablespoon finely chopped fresh tarragon

Salt and freshly milled black pepper, to taste

4–6 tablespoons unsalted butter, cut into bits

Make the risotto: Put the olive oil and onion in a heavy-bottomed pan over medium heat. Sweat the onion, stirring occasionally, until softened, and then stir in the rice. Slightly toast the rice, stirring slowly and carefully to prevent it from sticking. Add the bay leaf and deglaze with the wine, stirring to loosen the rice and onions. Cover the rice with a ladleful of vegetable stock and stir continuously until the rice absorbs all the stock. Repeat with more stock until the rice is al dente and creamy. It should be creamy but not runny. Stir in ½ cup Parmigiano and all the butter, reserving the remaining Parmigiano for garnish. Taste and season as needed with salt and pepper. Keep warm but do not cover.

Make the shrimp: Heat the oil and garlic in a heavy-bottomed sauté pan or skillet over medium heat. When it is sizzling hot, add the shrimp and sauté until pink and just cooked through. Remove from the pan and add the tomatoes and asparagus. Sauté until the asparagus is crisp tender. Add them to the shrimp and toss.

To plate: Divide the risotto among four heated dinner plates and arrange the shrimp and vegetables over the top. Return the sauté pan to medium-high heat and pour in the wine. Deglaze the pan, stirring and scraping the bottom, add lemon juice to taste, and stir in the tarragon. Let it boil until the wine is reduced by half. Season to taste with salt and pepper, remove the pan from the heat, and whisk in butter a few bits at a time until the sauce is thickened. Pour the sauce over the shrimp and risotto, sprinkle with the remaining Parmigiano, and serve immediately.

CHARLES J. RUSSO'S SEAFOOD

MARKET: 201 EAST 40TH STREET
RESTAURANT: 209 EAST 40TH STREET (NEXT DOOR)
(912) 234-5196
WWW.RUSSOSEAFOOD.COM
OWNER: CHARLES J. RUSSO JR.

Ask a native Savannahian where to buy the best and freshest local seafood, and the ready, sure answer will be "Why, Russo's, of course," usually accompanied by a look that casts doubt on your mental capacity. Founded by Charles J. and Antoinette Russo in 1946 and now run by son Charlie Jr., Russo's Seafood has set the standard for more than half a century.

Seafood runs deep with this family: Russo's mother was the daughter of A. C. Mathews, founder of a network of local seafood wholesalers. While the name may not suggest it, A. C. was Italian: his real name—Matteo Canerella—somehow got flip-flopped and anglicized by immigration officials. "We all had our niche," quips Charlie Jr. "The Jewish families had the groceries, we Italians had the fish markets."

However, it was with another seafood retailer, Louis Rayola, that the senior Russo learned his craft. He briefly left the business for a more secure job with the postal service, but after serving oversees as a noncommissioned postal officer during World War II, he felt the seafood business tugging at him. Together with his wife and young family, he opened his own retail shop on Waters Avenue in October of 1946. Their three children, Charlie Jr., Vincent, and Sarah, grew up in the business, which moved to its present location in 1970. After Charlie Jr. took the helm, his children, Charlie III and Kathleen Russo Coppage, grew up in the business as well, and they continue to be involved. In 2006, they expanded the business to include a restaurant in a rambling late-Victorian clapboard house next door to the market.

Of all the fish that Russo's sells, one of the most popular for locals is shad. A strictly seasonal luxury, it's only available between December and April, when the fish make their annual spawning run up the Ogeechee River. Shad, which is actually in the salmon family, is unfortunately as bony as it is popular, sporting three extra rows of fine bones on either side of the main spine. Only an experienced fishmonger can effectively fillet it without making the end result look as if two cats have fought over it.

Early in his career, Charlie Sr. befriended the Italian fishermen who followed the shad run up the coast from Georgia to Maine, and learned to neatly fillet a shad in less than five minutes. He passed the skill on to his son, and today wise Savannahians know to come to Russo's for their seasonal fix.

For many locals, however, the real point of this fish is less its distinctively flavored flesh than its roe. Russo's sells pairs of roe separately, and many locals enjoy it cooked alone, broiled in butter (as described below) and served over toast as a first course, broiled with bacon for breakfast, or poached with lemon and prepared exactly like sturgeon caviar.

Russo's Broiled Shad with Roe

(SERVES 4)

Now, back to that shad: Savannah cooks have devised a lot of elaborate recipes for this fish and its roe, but Russo rightly says there's no better way than to broil it, bathed in butter. The fish can of course be cooked without the roe, and, likewise, the roe is often broiled alone and served on buttered toast as an appetizer or breakfast dish. To cook only the roe as a first course, omit the fillets and allow two sets of roe for the same number of servings.

2 (¾-pound) shad fillets

1 set (about 6 ounces) shad roe, optional

3–4 tablespoons unsalted butter, melted

Juice of 2 lemons

Salt and freshly milled black pepper

Sweet paprika

Position a rack 10 inches below the heat source and preheat the broiler for 10 minutes. Rinse the shad and roes (if using) under cold running water and pat them dry.

Rub a broiler pan or rimmed baking sheet well with some melted butter and lay the shad fillets, skin side down, and the roe on it. Sprinkle with lemon juice, brush well with more melted butter, and season liberally with salt, pepper, and paprika.

Broil 10 inches below heat until cooked through, about 20 minutes. If cooking the roe, turn after 7 or 8 minutes, but do *not* turn the fish. Drizzle with the remaining butter and serve hot.

Russo's Deviled Crab
(SERVES 8)

Despite all the excitement around shad season, the year-round bestseller at Russo's, both in the market and across the way in the restaurant, is Antoinette Russo's Deviled Crab. A favorite with customers ever since she began making them more than sixty years ago, they're still faithfully made from her original recipe.

2 pounds blue-crab claw meat, or freshly picked meat from 2 dozen cooked blue crabs

4 tablespoons (½ stick) unsalted butter

½ cup finely chopped yellow onion

¼ cup finely chopped celery

¼ cup finely chopped bell pepper

2 large eggs

1½ sleeves Ritz Crackers, crushed

¼ cup tomato ketchup

2 tablespoons prepared mustard

2 tablespoons Worcestershire sauce

2 tablespoons Johnny Harris Barbecue Sauce (or your favorite brand)

1 tablespoon salt

½ tablespoon freshly milled pepper

Cayenne pepper, to taste

8 blue crab back-fin shells

Position a rack in the center of the oven and preheat it to 350°F. Pick over the crabmeat for bits of shell and set it aside. Melt the butter in a large skillet over medium heat. Add the onion, celery, and bell pepper and sauté, tossing often, until tender. Turn off the heat.

Break the eggs into a mixing bowl and lightly beat to mix. Add the crabmeat, onion, celery, and bell pepper. Stir in the crackers, ketchup, mustard, sauces, salt, pepper, and a dash or so of cayenne, to taste. Mix well and divide among the crab shells, mounding it on top. Bake until set and browned on top, about 30 minutes.

JOHNNY HARRIS BARBECUE SAUCE

Johnny Harris Barbecue Sauce is the original barbecue condiment from Johnny Harris Restaurant, an almost century-old Savannah institution specializing in seafood, fried chicken, and barbecue (and the only place where one can still get barbecued lamb, a vanishing Savannah specialty). Located at 1651 Victory Drive since the 1920s, its dining room remains popular with locals, and its sauce is a pantry mainstay. The original sauce (the version used by Russo's in their deviled crab above) has today been joined by several variations. They can be purchased at the restaurant, online at www.johnnyharris.com, or at a number of Savannah retailers, including Russo's.

Chef Joe Randall's Cooking School

5409 Waters Avenue
(912) 303-0409
www.chefjoerandall.com
Owner/Director: Chef Joe Randall

One can't help being reminded, on meeting Chef Joe Randall, of an old-fashioned Southern evangelist because, in a very real way, that is exactly what he is: a man with a gospel and a mission. The gospel is his native Southern cooking, and his mission is to spread it to any- and everyone that will open his or her mouth for a taste. Though classically trained, Chef Joe was weaned on Southern food and has been cooking it for his entire life. His passion for the cuisine is palpable and infectious. The cooking school's motto pretty much sums it up: "Put some South in your mouth." He believes so strongly in the beguiling power of Southern food that he's convinced all it will take is one taste to convert the most hardened doubter.

When Chef Joe came to Savannah in the late 1990s, it was to work as an executive chef for a local college. But gradually he began to notice that there were few options for home cooks who wanted to improve their skills. It also disturbed him that his beloved Southern cooking, particularly the local version of it, was getting so little respect. Since teaching was already in his blood, he decided to shift his culinary gears from professional cooking to education by opening a cooking school.

The trim little cottage that Chef Joe found for his school sits incongruously on a busy boulevard at the heart of the neighborhood surrounding Memorial Medical University Hospital, looking for all the world like a left-behind relic, because that's exactly what it is. A vintage cottage that was built when its surroundings were fields, pastures, and virgin woodlands well outside the city limits, today it is hemmed in by commercial buildings and medical office parks. Small and unassuming on the outside, inside everything about it is, like its owner, larger than life. Most of its interior partitions have been removed to make one large studio kitchen where students sit around a raised counter to watch and listen as Chef Joe, assisted by his lovely and charming wife, Barbara, spreads the good news of savory Southern cooking. The classes follow a lecture-demonstration format, in which the students mostly watch while the chef cooks and shares a wealth of knowledge that is born of nearly half a century of cooking.

Traditional Southern cooking is a blending of European and African foodways, and here in Savannah, which was once a major export center for rice when the grain was the primary money crop of the Lowcountry region, the cookery has distinct dishes that come straight out of the rice-growing regions of West Africa's Gold Coast. Chef Joe often features many of these traditional rice dishes, like this red rice pilau, supplemented with the fresh fish and shellfish that is abundant in its surrounding marshes and waterways.

Pan-Roasted Black Grouper
with Savannah Red Rice

(MAKES 8 SERVINGS)

8 (4-ounce) black grouper fillets

½ teaspoon salt

½ teaspoon freshly ground black pepper

2 tablespoons olive oil

6 tablespoons (¾ stick) unsalted butter, melted

For the Savannah red rice (makes 8 portions):

2 ounces salt pork, finely diced

½ cup diced red bell pepper

½ cup diced green bell pepper

¼ cup diced celery

1 cup diced onion

2 teaspoons minced garlic

¼ pound smoked sausage, diced

2 cups raw long-grain rice

2 cups canned whole tomatoes, crushed and drained

2 tablespoons tomato paste

1½ cups water

½ teaspoon salt

¼ teaspoon freshly ground black pepper

½ teaspoon ground cayenne pepper

2 tablespoons freshly squeezed lemon juice

¼ cup freshly chopped chives

Preheat the oven to 400°F. Season the grouper with salt and black pepper. Heat the olive oil and 2 tablespoons melted butter in a large skillet. Working in batches to avoid overcrowding, sear the grouper, skin side down, for 3 minutes, then turn and cook about 3 minutes longer, and place the pan in the preheated oven to finish, about 3 to 4 minutes more. Remove it from the oven and place the fillets on a heated platter and keep them warm. Repeat with the remaining grouper, adding the remaining butter as needed for each batch.

Make the red rice: Cook the salt pork until crisp in a large, heavy-bottomed saucepan. Add the red and green peppers, celery, onions, garlic, and sausage, and cook 3 to 4 minutes, or until the onion is translucent and the other vegetables softened. Add the rice and stir until it is well coated with the drippings. Stir in the tomatoes, tomato paste, water, salt, black pepper, and cayenne. Cover and simmer about 25 to 30 minutes or until rice is tender and the liquid is absorbed. Fluff the rice with a fork before serving.

To plate: Divide the red rice among eight warm dinner plates (Chef Joe shapes the rice by packing it into a ring mold) and top each portion with a grouper fillet. Sprinkle with lemon juice, garnish with freshly chopped chives, and serve immediately.

KITCHEN ACADEMICS

Ever since Leila Habersham, a young Civil War widow, opened a cooking school in the kitchen of her mother's home more than 150 years ago, Savannahians have been settling in to private and public kitchens, notebook and pencil in hand, for lessons in fine cooking. Almost a hundred years to the day later, the legendary Bailee Tenenbaum Kronowitz, a local artist and art collector, set a new trend for modern cooking classes when she followed in Mrs. Habersham's footsteps and began offering cooking classes in her home kitchen after being worn down by the persistent requests of friends who wanted to learn her secrets. Today, that trend continues to grow with Chef Joe Randall (page 48) in the lead, joined by a host of individuals and businesses that offer cooking classes either as a service for local customers or as a recreational opportunity for visitors.

Kitchenware Outfitters of Savannah
Twelve Oaks Shopping Center
5500 Abercorn Street, Suite 18
(912) 356-1117
www.kitchenwareoutfitters.com
Owners: Barbara and David Freeman
Director: Chef Damon Lee Fowler

Owners David and Barbara Freeman like to think of Kitchenware Outfitters as a hardware store for kitchens. Stocking everything from knives, wooden spoons, and whisks to pots, pans, and electric mixers, this full-service store also offers after-hours cooking classes in a full studio kitchen at the rear of the sales floor. Directed by cookbook author and cooking teacher Damon Lee Fowler, the school's instructors include popular local chefs as well as nationally celebrated chefs and cookbook authors. Though most classes follow a lecture/demonstration format, there are occasional hands-on classes, and students are always welcome to come into the kitchen and try their hand at a new technique.

Kitchens on the Square
38 Barnard Street
(912) 236-0100
www.kitchensonthesquare.com
Owner/Director: Nicole Carrillo

This kitchen specialty store, just off newly restored Ellis Square and around the corner from Paula Deen's The Lady & Sons (page 90), lives by the slogan "Make your kitchen smile." You won't find pots and pans here: Owner Nicole Carrillo instead calls it a mini amusement park for food lovers and has put the emphasis on unusual vintage and decorative kitchenware, offering many of the tools, pottery, and other equipment used by The Lady herself. Kitchens on the Square also offers intimate cooking classes in a studio kitchen at the back of the salesroom, both after hours and in a popular "lunch and learn" format at midday on Friday and Saturday.

700 Kitchen Cooking School
Mansion on Forsyth Park
(912) 721-5006
www.mansiononforsythpark.com
Owner: The Kessler Collection
Director: Chef Darin Sehnert

One of the most popular amenities at this downtown luxury hotel, aside from its fine restaurant 700 Drayton (see page 2), is the 700 Kitchen Cooking School under the direction of veteran chef and culinary instructor Darin Sehnert. A Johnson & Wales graduate who has cooked across the globe from his native Southern California to London, Chef Sehnert has taught for such prestigious culinary programs as the California campus of Le Cordon Bleu–Paris and the Disney Institute in Orlando, Florida. The 700 Kitchen Cooking School is a modern, fully appointed studio that offers hands-on classes both mornings and evenings to individuals and groups and for corporate team-building programs.

Chocolat by Adam Turoni

323 West Broughton Street
(570) 510 1820
www.chocolatat.com
Chef/Owner: Adam Turoni, Chocolatier

When people meet master chocolatier Adam Turoni, whether at his new chocolate shop or just by bumping into him on the street, they are immediately struck by the warmth and passion with which this young man approaches life in general—and chocolate in particular. There have been many influences that have shaped this passion: his father, who instilled his work ethic and enthusiasm for living; the legendary Alice Waters, with whom he apprenticed at Chez Panisse; his professors at The Culinary Institute of America in Hyde Park, New York. But the person he really credits with instilling his love for the alchemy of cooking and baking is his grandmother. He explains, "When we were growing up, we'd have sleepovers at my grandmother's. Everyone else would go to bed and my grandmother and I would be baking cookies all night. That intimate setting—just us, quiet, making cookies—that is what made me want to be a cook and a baker."

Adam fell in love with chocolate making while studying at The Culinary Institute when he and a handful of others began to study the craft privately with one of their professors. "I'd get up really early and go in to the school, and there we'd be, just a couple of us at five a.m., making chocolate with our professor, drinking our espresso, a little music in the background. It was so peaceful—and so much like those times with my grandmother. It's still the way I work best: early in the morning, just me, a little music, my coffee, and the chocolate."

After he finished school, Adam came to Savannah and happened into Wright Square Cafe (see page 180). There he recognized a similar passion for chocolate in owner Gary Hall and offered to make a signature line of chocolates for the cafe. Those chocolates, and Adam, were an immediate hit. But as their popularity bloomed, he quickly outgrew the limited work space at the cafe, and rented a studio in the Starland Dairy District where he had room to work, at first selling exclusively to Wright Square. As the business grew to include several clients, however, he realized that he missed the direct contact with the consumer. "There is nothing to equal that feeling you get as you watch someone choose a chocolate and take a bite—that look of initial surprise and then utter bliss that comes over their face. That is just so rewarding."

He found a space on Broughton Street, took a deep breath, and decided to make the plunge. The chocolates are beautiful, almost too beautiful to eat, and handsomely presented; Adam knows that presentation is key, but the really beguiling thing about them is that the flavors seem hauntingly familiar. That's because he is not the least interested in reinventing the wheel or in bowling people over with some clever new chocolate that no one has ever done before. He loves playing with familiar ideas—almond bark, a peanut butter cup, rich dark chocolate tablets filled with honey—and tries to make it not unique, but better.

Fig & Cognac Truffles

(MAKES ABOUT 65 TRUFFLES)

This fig and cognac truffle is something of a signature for Adam. It's one of the first that he ever made and remains one of his favorites.

5 ounces heavy cream

16 ounces finely chopped dark chocolate

11 ounces fig preserves

2½ ounces cognac

6 ounces unsweetened cocoa powder

Special Equipment: parchment paper, latex gloves

Line a 9 X 13-inch baking pan with parchment paper. Pour the cream into a saucepan and bring to a boil. Remove the pan from the heat. Add the chopped chocolate to the cream and stir the mixture until it is smooth and homogeneous. If all the chocolate pieces don't melt, place the pan back on the burner, being extremely careful not to burn the chocolate. Stir until smooth. Add the fig preserves and cognac and mix until incorporated. Pour the mixed ganache onto the parchment-covered baking pan and cover with plastic wrap. Refrigerate until the ganache is firm (about 1 hour).

Remove the pan from the refrigerator and place the ganache in a mixing bowl fitted with a paddle attachment. Mix for 30 seconds. Once mixed, allow the ganache to rest at room temperature for 5 to 10 minutes. Once the ganache is ready to be shaped, spoon out individual balls onto a sheet pan lined with parchment. At this stage the ganache must be firm to work with: It should feel as firm as play dough or have a claylike consistency. If the ganache is too loose, place it back in the refrigerator and wait until it hardens.

Place the cocoa powder in a bowl. Using latex gloves roll each truffle into a small, smooth ball. Once all the truffles are shaped, add a stem onto each truffle by placing your thumb and two fingers over the top quarter of the truffle and pinch lightly while pulling up. Once the stem is made, place each truffle in the cocoa powder, coating it fully, and deposit it on the tray, sitting them upright so that the stems point upward. Using a butter knife, I lightly indent all side of the truffles starting with my knife at the bottom of the truffle, and working my way up to the stem in a straight line. This final procedure helps the truffle resemble a realistic fig.

Hazelnut Crème

(MAKES ABOUT 3 CUPS)

If you love chocolate-nut spreads such as Nutella, Adam says this hazelnut crème is for you: Easy to make, even easier to eat, it will keep for more than a month. Use it not only as a spread, but as a filling for sandwich cookies or pastries. At his shop, Adam turns it into a crunchy center for a truffle that has become one of the most popular in the shop.

3 cups hazelnuts
½ cup confectioners' sugar
5 ounces milk or dark chocolate
2 pinches salt

Preheat the oven to 375°F. Place the hazelnuts on a baking sheet and roast the nuts until they resemble a golden brown color. Remove the nuts from the oven and lightly rub them with a towel to remove as much of the brown skin as you can. Don't worry about getting it all.

Immediately place the nuts into a food processor along with the confectioners' sugar. Grind the hazelnut-sugar mixture until the ground hazelnuts convert into a smooth liquid puree (about 5 to 10 minutes). During this process the hazelnuts turn from ground nuts into a smooth creamy liquid that will be extremely hot. When the hazelnut crème is smooth, add the chopped chocolate and salt and mix until it is fully incorporated.

Transfer the chocolate-hazelnut crème into a separate bowl, allowing it to cool. Once the mixture cools to room temperature, stir vigorously for 1 minute and deposit it into glass canning jars. Seal the jars and store the filling at room temperature. The jarred hazelnut crème can last anywhere from 2 to 4 months when stored properly.

If the mixture is too hard to spread, place in the microwave and heat briefly to soften, or in the future, reduce the amount of chocolate added to change the consistency.

Modern Pumpkin Truffle

Passion Fruit Truffle

White chocolate ganache infused with passion fruit and splashed with color incased in a crisp white chocolate shell.
$1.95 each

Circa 1875 Gastro Pub

48 Whitaker Street
(912) 443-1875
www.circa1875.com
Owners: Jeffery Downey and Donald Lubowcki
Executive Chef: David Landrigan

The story behind Circa 1875, an elegant, old-fashioned downtown restaurant and pub, is one of two loves. When owning partners Jeffery Downey and Donald Lubowcki first visited Savannah, they fell in love with the city almost on sight. But logistics got in their way and, deciding it wasn't in the cards, they tried living somewhere else. Savannah, however, had her hooks into them, and before long, they began making plans to move back for good. They found a house, got jobs in the hospitality industry, and began to dream of opening a restaurant of their own.

In the interim, the two visited France, and that's where the other love comes into the picture—the neighborhood bistro/pubs found all over Paris. They knew that when they did open their restaurant, that was what they wanted it to be—a cozy neighborhood hangout where one could get everything from a light, inexpensive supper and beer to a celebratory five-course dinner with wine. When they discovered that the pub at the back of this handsome post–Civil War building was available, they took one look and knew that this was exactly the place for the kind of restaurant they wanted to create. Putting the restoration of their 1920s Ardsley Park home on hold, they dove in with both feet and opened in 2007, just in time for Savannah's infamous St. Patrick's Day celebration, the third largest in the country. The holiday can make or break a new downtown restaurant; fortunately, it made Circa 1875.

Though the name comes from the year the building was built, it's doubly appropriate since the owners have consciously tried to preserve and enhance the original fabric, creating a small trip back in time to those French neighborhood restaurant-pubs that were in their golden age back when this building was new. As it happens, the space had actually been a pub in 1875, and luckily a lot of its original detailing had survived. A little forensic work uncovered the original colors, and they were able to match them. With its original pressed-tin ceiling, cornice, and beaded-board walls sporting a fresh coat of their original colors, period mosaic-tiled floor, Belle Époque style furniture, and a gilded antique cash register completing the effect, the pub has the settled look of a Parisian tavern that has been around for more than a century. The dining room's period lighting, bentwood cafe chairs, and gilt mirrors remain consistent with the theme.

In the capable hands of Executive Chef David Landrigan, the cuisine nods back to the classic French bistro cookery, and yet it is fresh and forward-looking. Calling food "the great communicator," Chef Landrigan declines to philosophize about it, preferring to let the dish speak for itself. Of his own style, he simply sums it up with shrug and "I just love cooking—that's it."

Pan-Seared Carolina Brook Trout with Roasted Provençal Vegetables, Lemon-Caper Brown Butter Sauce & Fresh Herbs

(SERVES 4)

For the roasted Provençal vegetables:

1 medium rutabaga, peeled and diced
1 medium carrot, peeled and diced
½ pound parsnips, peeled and diced
2–4 tablespoons extra-virgin olive oil
Salt and freshly milled black pepper
1–2 tablespoons herbes de Provence, to taste
¾ pound yellow squash, seeded and diced
¾ pound zucchini squash, seeded and diced
4 ounces grape tomatoes, cleaned and halved
1 head garlic cloves, peeled but left whole
4 medium mushrooms (cremini, white button, or portobello), cleaned and quartered
1 tablespoon chopped fresh marjoram

For the trout:

4 Carolina brook trout, filleted and butterflied
2 cups all-purpose flour
2 cups cornmeal
Salt and freshly milled black pepper to taste
6–8 tablespoons clarified butter or cooking oil

For the lemon-caper brown butter sauce
   (makes about 1 cup):

4 tablespoons clarified butter
2 shallots, minced
4–6 ounces capers, drained and rinsed, to taste
⅓ cup white wine
Juice of ½ lemon
6 tablespoons (¾ stick) unsalted butter
2–3 tablespoon fresh Italian (flat-leaf) parsley chopped

Make the roasted Provençal vegetables: Preheat the oven to 345°F. Keeping the rutabaga, carrots, and parsnips separate from the other vegetables, toss them in a little olive oil and season with salt, pepper, and herbes de Provence. Spread them on a rimmed sheet pan in an even layer and roast 15 to 17 minutes.

Repeat the same process with the squashes, roasting for 10 to 12 minutes, then with the tomatoes and garlic and roast them for 10 to 12 minutes. Finally, repeat the process with the mushrooms also roasting them 10 to 12 minutes.

Note: Keeping the different types of vegetables separate is important because moisture will leach out of the squashes and mushrooms; if they are combined too early, it will result in a soggy mess.

Combine all of the vegetables, adjust the seasoning, and keep warm until ready to serve. Just before serving, finish with chopped marjoram.

Prepare the trout: Clean the trout, removing any remaining pin bones. Combine the flour and cornmeal in a wide, shallow bowl and season with salt and pepper.

In a large skillet, heat the clarified butter or oil over medium-high heat. Place the trout flesh side down into the flour-cornmeal mixture, make sure it is evenly coated, turn, and repeat on the skin side. Shake off any excess and gently place the trout flesh side down into the skillet for about 2 to 3 minutes or until the flesh is nice and golden brown. Carefully flip over to the skin side and cook for an additional 2 to 3 minutes. Work in batches, if necessary.

Remove trout and drain cooking oil/butter, blot on absorbent paper, and transfer to warm serving plates.

Divide the roasted vegetables among the serving plates.

Make the sauce: Wipe out the skillet in which the trout cooked and put it back over medium heat. Add the clarified butter and let it melt. Add the shallots and cook until translucent, then add the

capers and white wine, bring to a boil, and let it boil until reduced by half.

Add the lemon juice and let it continue reducing for about 1 minute. Add the whole butter and let it melt. Cook until the sauce begins to caramelize; it should have a nutty aroma. Swirl the parsley into the sauce and either pour it over the trout immediately or pour it into a warmed sauce boat for family-style dining.

CLARY'S CAFE

404 ABERCORN STREET
(912) 233-0402
WWW.CLARYSCAFE.COM
OWNER: JAN WILSON

For decades, the soda fountain of Clary's Drug Store was an institution for downtown Savannahians—a place to stop for fountain drinks, ice cream, or a quick glass of sweet tea, and *the* place to meet your neighbors for breakfast or a chicken salad sandwich. It was not long on decor: In fact, to call its scarred plywood paneling, patched Naugahyde-covered stools and chairs, and faded melamine counters "decor" would have been a real stretch. But none of that seemed to matter to those in the neighborhood. Nothing here ever changed, and they didn't want it to. But when the drugstore's owners decided to close the soda fountain, change was inevitable. It was taken over by veteran restaurateur John Nichol and partner Linda Davis, who overhauled the kitchen and transformed the drab, rundown soda fountain into a stylish cafe. A few years later, when the drugstore closed, Nichol and Davis expanded the cafe into the rest of the building. Eventually, they moved their business to City Market, and Clary's was taken over by new owners who returned the cafe to its original soda fountain/ breakfast-lunch counter format.

Then something happened that changed everything. The old Clary's Drug Store soda fountain was featured in John Berendt's best-selling book *Midnight in the Garden of Good and Evil*. Overnight, the little cafe became the destination for hundreds of curious visitors who didn't care that what they saw was not the timeworn soda fountain of an old neighborhood pharmacy, but a neat little neighborhood cafe. It was Clary's—and that was all they needed to know.

Now owned by Jan Wilson, who had formerly managed the cafe for its previous owners, Clary's remains haunted—not by ghosts, as so many of its neighbors claim to be—but by its *Midnight* reputation. While it continues to be a popular breakfast and lunch stop for downtowners, its bread and butter is the steady stream of curiosity seekers who want a little taste of the Old Savannah that Berendt captured.

The Crab Shack

40 Estill Hammock Road
Tybee Island
(912) 786-9857
www.thecrabshack.com
Owners: Belinda and Jack Flanigan

The Crab Shack is without a doubt one of the most organic restaurants in Savannah—and that's not a reference to its laid-back, casual outdoor setting: It's how it happened. When its owners, Captains Belinda and Jack Flanigan, bought the small cinder-block marina and fishing camp on a bluff along Tybee Island's Chimney Creek thirty years ago, they had little idea of establishing a local culinary landmark. They were only looking for a way to simplify their lives and come back home to their native Lowcountry. For a couple of years, they operated the fishing camp and marina while studying for their captain's licenses, hoping to add chartered fishing expeditions to the business.

The Crab Shack began with impromptu gatherings after those expeditions started, when fishing camp patrons and locals began to gather around a picnic table on the dock to cool off and relax with a cold beer, watch the spectacular sunsets, and stuff themselves on Captain Jack's boiled crab and shrimp that had been caught in crab traps sunk off the dock and in shrimp nets pulled behind the charter fishing boats. These casual gatherings bloomed into a very casual restaurant in 1987, with Jack cooking the seafood and Belinda waiting tables. The first menu—still on display in the dining area—was scrawled onto a four-by-eight sheet of marine plywood, and the tables were covered with old newspaper. As the restaurant continued to grow table by table, this

being Savannah, locals began asking for drinks, so the Flanigans applied for a liquor license and had what Jack calls "an old-fashioned bar raising." Today, in addition to dozens of tables covering a rambling deck shaded by sprawling live oaks, palms, and banana trees, there's a shed-covered dining area and bar, a gift shop where patrons can buy Captain Crab's Secret Spice blend, hot pepper sauce, and seafood cocktail sauce, an aviary, and—believe it or not—pet gators.

CAPTAIN CRAB'S LOWCOUNTRY BOIL

(SERVES 8)

Boiled crab, spiked with Captain Jack's proprietary spice blend, is obviously still a mainstay of The Crab Shack menu, but equally popular is this traditional Lowcountry dish of shrimp poached with potatoes, corn, onions, and spicy smoked sausage. Found throughout the region, from Frogmore, South Carolina, where it is believed to have been created, all the way down to the coast of northern Florida and up to the Outer Banks of North Carolina, it varies a little from cook to cook, but the primary elements are always the same. Here is the Crab Shack's signature version.

½ cup **Captain Crab's Secret Spice**
   (or any seafood seasoning)
¼ cup salt
4 tablespoons freshly ground black pepper
¼ cup white vinegar
2 pounds new potatoes
2 pounds smoked sausage links, cut into 1-inch pieces
8 ears corn, shucked and cut into 3-inch pieces
½ onion, cut into thin slices (optional)
3 pounds fresh shrimp, tails on
2–3 lemons, each cut into 8 wedges
Seafood cocktail sauce

Put 8 quarts water into a 16-quart pot and bring it to a rolling boil. Add the Captain Crab's Secret Spice, salt, pepper, and vinegar. Add the new potatoes and cook for 5 minutes. Add the sausage, corn, and onion, if using, bring it back to a simmer, and continue cooking until the potatoes are tender, about 10 minutes. Turn off the heat, add the shrimp, cover, and let it sit for 2 minutes. The residual heat will be enough to cook the shrimp. They will float to the top, and their shells will begin to separate from the meat.

Drain, sprinkle everything with additional Secret Spice to taste, and serve with lemon wedges, cocktail sauce, and plenty of paper towels.

CITY MARKET

From its founding in 1733, Ellis Square was the hub of Savannah's historic market district. Its importance waned in the early twentieth century, however, and suffered a crushing blow in 1955 with the demolition of its historic heart, the mid-nineteenth century Romanesque Revival market pavilion that had for nearly a century filled Ellis Square. The loss of this significant structure was the catalyst that galvanized preservationists and launched Savannah's National Landmark Historic District, but for years, the market district itself, especially the core four-block area flanking St. Julian Street, languished. Fortunately, its anchoring squares, Ellis and Franklin, have been beautifully restored, and the brick-paved street has been restricted to a pedestrian mall. The area is once again a thriving part of downtown commerce and is flanked by charming sidewalk cafes that comprise some of downtown's significant restaurants, from The City Market Café, the original sidewalk cafe at its eastern end, to Vinnie Van Go-Go's Pizza (where locals go for their Italian pie fix) and upscale Belford's Seafood and Steaks (page 21) at its western end. One street over, but still a part of the district, is Mollie McPherson's Pub & Grill (which offers hearty, delicious pub food and a scotch list longer than your arm) and Garibaldi Cafe (see page 80), making City Market one of the most significant dining hubs in town.

Crystal Beer Parlor

301 West Jones Street (Corner of Jones and Jefferson)
(912) 349-1000
WWW.CRYSTALBEERPARLOR.COM
Chef/Owner: John Nichols

While the name of this Savannah icon may invite images of smoky backroom poker, "The Crystal," as locals know it, has really been a family cafe specializing in serious comfort food ever since it first opened in 1933. While it was indeed one of the first restaurants in the country to serve alcoholic beverages after the repeal of Prohibition, it's more of a neighborhood gathering place than saloon, and for many downtowners, it's the site for many a rite of passage, from first dates, to engagements, to golden wedding anniversaries.

From the look of its interior, with its original Art Deco bar and tall red-leatherette booths, framed vintage newspaper clippings, posters, and lazily spinning paddle fans, it would seem that nothing much has changed since its first day in business. It in fact seems so permanent and eternal that it's hard to imagine that it was very nearly lost. After falling onto rocky times in the late 1990s, this iconic tavern changed hands several times and eventually closed its doors—from the look of it, for good. Fortunately, veteran restaurateur John Nichols refused to believe that the beer parlor had reached its last chapter. Enlisting his brother Philip, he rescued and refurbished the building, carefully preserving its 1930s pub atmosphere, and reopened.

Chef Nichols is proud that the core kitchen staff has been with the Crystal for more than thirty years, and has been careful to see that the menu retains most of the legendary original fare—house-made chili, Savannah-style gumbo, creamy crab stew, hand-cut fries and potato chips, fried seafood, burgers, and chili dogs—all made from the original recipes by cooks who have been making them for decades. But he has also revitalized the fare by adding Greek-accented dishes from his own family, and updated daily specials that feature local seafood and produce.

GREEK TACOS

(SERVES 4)

One of the revitalized family dishes is the Greek Taco, a cross between the classic gyro wrap and a soft-tortilla taco. It's made with house-made warm, juicy Greek lamb loaf and served on a hot toasted pita topped with shredded lettuce, tomato, and onion, exactly like a taco, but the flavor is all Eastern Mediterranean. Have it with the house-made potato chips for a real taste of the old and new Crystal.

For the tsadziki sauce (makes about 3½ cups):

3½ cups plain Greek yogurt
Salt
1 cup peeled, seeded, and finely chopped cucumber
1 clove garlic, crushed
2 teaspoons olive oil
1 tablespoon dried dill
1 tablespoon freshly squeezed lemon juice

For the Greek lamb loaf (serves 8–10):

2 large eggs, lightly beaten
½ cup whole milk
½ cup plain bread crumbs
1 tablespoon minced garlic
2 tablespoons crumbled dried oregano
2 tablespoons crumbled dried basil
1⅛ teaspoons salt
¾ teaspoon freshly milled pepper
2½ pounds ground lamb
1½ pounds ground chuck

For the tacos:

4 whole pita bread rounds
Olive oil
1 pound warm Greek lamb loaf, sliced as thinly
    as possible
About 1 cup tsadziki sauce
1 cup shredded or chopped romaine or iceberg lettuce
1 cup diced ripe tomato
1 cup small-dice red or yellow onion
About ½–⅔ cup crumbled feta cheese

Make the sauce: Line a wire mesh strainer with a clean kitchen towel. Mix together the yogurt and 1 teaspoon salt and turn it into the prepared strainer. Set it over a bowl and let it drain for 2 hours. Meanwhile, lightly sprinkle the cucumber with salt and let it stand 15 minutes, then gently press it dry. Combine it with the strained yogurt, garlic, oil, dill, and lemon juice, and mix well. Cover and refrigerate until chilled.

Make the Greek lamb loaf: Position a rack in the middle of the oven and preheat to 375°F. Blend together the eggs, milk, bread crumbs, garlic, herbs, salt, and pepper in a large mixing bowl. Crumble the ground meat into it and combine, mixing well. Place the mixture in a loaf pan or turn it out onto a rimmed baking sheet and shape into an oval. Bake about 1 hour, or until the internal temperature reaches 160°F. Let rest 15 minutes before slicing.

Make the tacos: Brush the pita bread lightly with olive oil and warm it in a skillet or heavy sauté pan over medium heat, turning once. When hot and beginning to toast (but still soft), remove and place on a serving plate.

Lay 4 ounces warm lamb loaf over the middle of each pita and drizzle with approximately ¼ cup tsadziki sauce. Top with lettuce, tomato, onion, and feta, and serve immediately.

Elizabeth on 37th

105 East 37th Street
(912) 236-5547
www.elizabethon37th.net
Owners: Elizabeth Terry, Greg and
Gary Butch
Executive Chef: Kelly Yambor

A true Savannah landmark since its opening in 1981, James Beard award–winning chef Elizabeth Terry's restaurant, Elizabeth on 37th, needs no introduction. But what you may not know about this iconic dining room, located in a graceful Edwardian-era mansion surrounded by lush herb gardens, is that it began its life as a modest dessert cafe. It was not long, however, before Terry, a leading advocate for regional American cookery, began to expand her menu and build a national reputation with her elegant reinterpretations of traditional Southern fare. In just a few years, the restaurant, with its refined, warm atmosphere, knowledgeable and well-trained yet friendly waitstaff, and one of the best wine lists in the entire Southeast, had blossomed into something of a culinary mecca.

Yet for all its reputation, Elizabeth on 37th has never lost the feel of a family restaurant, and guests still remark that dining here feels like being a guest in someone's home. That's partly because Terry's vision and legacy have passed into the capable hands of Greg and Gary Butch, brothers who have been working with her from the beginning. Partners in the restaurant since 1988, they took over the management after Terry retired from the kitchen and brought in Executive Chef Kelly Yambor. Perhaps the best example of the family atmosphere they strive to maintain is their celebration of the midwinter holidays: For three nights in late December, guests are treated to a sumptuous prix-fixe menu that includes complimentary rounds of house-made (and appropriately named) "Gregarious" eggnog and carols performed by the Holiday Harmonies, a local singing group.

While sharing Terry's original vision and remaining true to her "nouvelle Southern" style, Chef Yambor has gone in her own direction. The menu still features a few of the original signature dishes like Terry's Spicy Savannah Red Rice with Georgia Shrimp, Grouper Celeste, and Savannah Cream Cake, but Yambor has expanded on the theme and asserted some of her own style, taking advantage of the extensive herb garden surrounding the restaurant and featuring local, fresh, seasonal ingredients.

Firefly Cafe

321 Habersham Street (at Troupe Square)
(912) 234-1971
www.fireflycafega.com

The garden level of the mid-nineteenth-century residence overlooking Troupe Square from the corner of Habersham and Harris Streets has had an important role in Savannah's culinary history. Built in 1869 for John McDonough, a former mayor of Savannah, the home's ground-floor service area became a grocery after the house was acquired in 1946 by Italian immigrant Alfio Finocchiaro, and remained the neighborhood's primary market until it closed in 1969. Its next long-term tenant was specialty butcher Triple T Meats, which was for many years one of downtown's top purveyors of quality beef, pork, and poultry until it, too, fell victim to a shifting market and closed in the late 1980s. Shortly afterward, the first cafe to occupy the space opened and was rapidly followed by half a dozen others that quickly came and went until Firefly Cafe opened in 2002.

Quickly building a reputation with its weekend brunches, Firefly has become a neighborhood institution, offering a reliable menu of eclectic, urban-modern, cafe-style fare—fresh salads, seasonal soups, local seafood, and pasta. Though its dining room is small and a few steps below street level, tall windows to the south and east ensure that it is bright and inviting on all but the cloudiest of days, making the room seem gracious, open, and more spacious than it is. However, it is not the sunny dining room that is Firefly's most popular seating, but the oak- and magnolia-shaded sidewalk tables along Habersham Street. Troupe Square, known by locals as the "dog square," has always been something of an outdoor living room for the neighborhood, where dog-walking neighbors meet in the cool of the evening to visit and catch up on gossip, drink in one hand and leash in the other. Not surprisingly, pets are welcome at Firefly's outdoor tables, and Troupe Square residents freely stop to mingle with friends from other neighborhoods. Only a torrential summer rain seems to empty these seats.

Ele Fine Fusion

7815 US Highway 80 East
Wilmington Island
(912) 898-2221
www.elesavannah.com
Owner/Executive Chef: Sean Thongsiri
Co-Owner: Ele Tran

As patrons turn into the forecourt of Ele Fine Fusion, the Pan-Asian restaurant on US Highway 80 in Wilmington Island, it feels almost as if they have suddenly left the Georgia Lowcountry behind and landed in front of one of Los Angeles's cutting-edge nightspots. The dramatically lit landscaping and central fountain, the serene, modern stone and stucco facade, and the subtle, backlit signage all lend an urbane California elegance to what is essentially a family-run neighborhood restaurant. Born in Saigon, Vietnam, to a family of entrepreneurs who have taught her the importance of common sense and careful attention to detail, co-owner Ele Tran has been in the restaurant business for most of her life, and her family has long been an important, if quietly unseen, presence in Savannah's restaurant scene. With a keen eye for quality, understated elegance, and detail, Ele sees that the handsome dining room meets her exacting standards, while her partner, Executive Chef Sean Thongsiri, makes sure that the kitchen meets his own standards for authenticity, freshness, and careful preparation. After years of development, Thongsiri and Tran took the most influential aspects of their upbringings, blended them into one, and are now sharing it one handcrafted dish at a time.

The currently fashionable farm-to-table idea is nothing new to Chef Sean; it runs deep in his blood. He grew up in the kitchen with his grandmother in Vientiane, Laos, and her cooking really began in the market. Only satisfied with the freshest and choicest ingredients, she spent as much time in the open-air markets of Vientiane as she did in her kitchen. It was there, watching his grandmother interact with the farmers, fishermen, and merchants who brought their freshly harvested produce directly to the consumers, that Chef Sean learned the importance of forming strong relationships with those who provisioned his family's table. And it's a practice that he has conscientiously continued to this day. While he still cooks within the traditions that were laid down for him by his grandmother, he loves to improvise and push the envelope with new ingredients, and to combine the traditions and cuisines both of Southeast Asia and his adopted home in America.

Spicy Steak with Crisp Vegetables & Homemade Curry

(SERVES 4)

1 pound flank steak

4 teaspoons red chile paste

4 teaspoons coconut milk

4 teaspoons oyster sauce

4 teaspoons sugar

4 teaspoons fish sauce

1 tablespoon cooking oil

4 teaspoons crushed, minced garlic

2 cups mixed prepared and sliced vegetables such as bamboo shoots, green onion, red and green bell peppers, white or yellow onion, snow peas

Lettuce leaves, for serving

Cilantro sprigs, for garnish (optional)

4 cups hot steamed aromatic rice, such as jasmine

Thinly slice the steak across the grain. Combine the chile paste, coconut milk, oyster sauce, sugar, and fish sauce in a small bowl. Heat a wok over high heat and drizzle in the oil. Add the garlic and toss until fragrant. Add the steak and stir fry for a minute or until it loses its raw, red color. Add the combined sauce ingredients and continue to stir-fry for another minute or 2, then add the vegetables and stir fry for another 2 to 3 minutes. Line four serving plates with lettuce leaves and divide the spicy steak among them. Garnish with cilantro, if desired, and serve at once with rice.

SOUTHERN SWISS DAIRY, LLC

279 ROSIER ROAD
WAYNESBORO, GA 30830
(706) 830-3937
WWW.SOUTHERNSWISSDAIRY.COM
OWNERS: JIMMY AND GINNY FRANKS

"This is an eight-day-a-week job," says Jimmy Franks of Southern Swiss Dairy, the farm that he and his wife, Ginny, own and operate in Waynesboro, Georgia. "Christmas morning isn't any different from any other day. The cows have got to be milked every morning at four o'clock no matter what."

Of course, the Franks, who both have the farming life in their blood (Ginny is a fifth-generation dairywoman), already knew it wasn't going to be easy. But they also knew it to be very satisfying and never put a thought to doing anything different. For years they ran a conventional dairy farm, tending cows and selling the milk to a co-op for processing. But by 2008, wildly fluctuating milk prices were making it difficult to break even, and the future of their farm and its twenty-year-old herd of Brown Swiss cows was uncertain.

Since giving up the farm was unthinkable, they looked for alternatives and decided that their best option was to open their own processing and bottling facility and sell directly to the public. Determined to provide only the freshest and most healthful milk, cream, and butter, they also made the decision not to homogenize. Though this process, which changes the molecular structure of the fat so that it stays suspended in the liquid, does help prolong shelf life and make the milk convenient for consumers (it doesn't have to be shaken to redistribute the cream), there are growing concerns about its healthfulness. Naming the dairy "Southern Swiss" after their beloved Brown Swiss cows, they opened in 2010.

"Our biggest challenge," says Jimmy Franks, "has been educating our customers about that cream at the top. They're not used to it, and when they see it, they just freak out, thinking their milk is spoiled."

Initial growth was slow: At first they were selling only from their plant and at farmers' markets across the region, but then they began to attract the attention of a few select retailers. Their biggest break was being discovered by the region's chefs, who were eager to incorporate top-quality local products in their cooking. Today their products are used in most of Savannah's top restaurants, and locals can buy them at Brighter Day (see The Hippie Grocers, page 89) and the Forsyth Farmers' Market (see Market Fresh, page 101). Southern Swiss also supplies Georgia-based cheesemaker Flat Creek Lodge and Atlanta Fresh Creamery, makers of high-quality Greek-style yogurt.

Gryphon Tea Room

337 Bull Street
(912) 525-5880
Owner: Savannah College of Art and Design

Though not the oldest of Savannah's many squares, in many ways Madison Square is one of its most historic. The site is not only where the Revolutionary War Battle for Savannah was fought, it also boasts many of the city's most significant monuments. At its center, appropriately, is the monument to Revolutionary War hero Sergeant William Jasper, and surrounding it are the Green-Meldrim Mansion, which played a significant role during the Civil War as General Sherman's headquarters; St. John's Episcopal Church, whose imposing Gothic spire houses a forty-two-bell carillon; the Romanesque Revival Savannah Volunteer Guard, which later became the flagship building for The Savannah College of Art and Design (see sidebar on page 146); E. Shaver Booksellers, one of the Southeast's largest and oldest independent book dealers; and, finally, the colorful Beaux Arts–style Scottish Rite temple building, whose main corner was for many years home to Solomon's Drug Store.

Solomon's and its soda fountain were a neighborhood institution, but part of its significance today is that through all its years of operation, the store was never redecorated, so when it closed, most of its original fixtures, from the mosaic tile floor, wood paneling, shelving, and hand-labeled druggist's drawers, to decorative stained-glass panels, mirrors, and, significantly, a gryphon-ornamented clock, were still in place—and in mint condition.

Today, the old drugstore is preserved and honored as the Gryphon Tea Room, an old-fashioned English-style tearoom owned by The Savannah College of Art and Design. At first, because of its proximity to the college's flagship building, the college made use of the space as a student canteen, but as the campus grew and expanded across the Historic District, the founders felt that there were better ways to use this historic space, and the canteen was transformed into a tearoom for the entire community to enjoy. Named for that gryphon-ornamented clock, its decor takes its inspiration both from the English tearooms on which it was modeled and from the appointments of this historic interior.

The decor may be old-fashioned, but the menu is fresh and current. It changes periodically; however, its mainstay is tea, carefully brewed (like the decor) the old-fashioned way: in a heated pot with loose tea leaves.

FORM Cheesecake, Wine, and Gourmet-To-Go

1801 Habersham Street
WWW.FORM-CWG.COM
(912) 236-7642
Executive Chef/Owner: Claude Auerbach
Chef/Owner: Brian Torres
Baker/Owner: Jimmy Kleinschmidt

The first thing to know about FORM is that it is not a restaurant.

"A restaurant gets you in a rut," says Brian Torres, one of FORM's partners who had previously operated a popular neighborhood restaurant (Eos) in this same 1950s modern brick bank building. "No matter how good it is—you make the same fantastic steak with the same sauce that your customers love, night after night. Here we can spread our wings. Last year we did something like two hundred private dinners, not including the catering—and each one was unique—totally original."

After the restaurant closed in 2010, Torres wanted to stay in food service but was pretty sure he didn't want to try another restaurant, so he got together with friends Claude Auerbach and Jimmy Kleinschmidt and a fourth man who is no longer involved. Bringing a combined experience of more than one hundred years in fine food and wine to the table, they drew on each partner's strengths, and the concept for the present business—if you will excuse the expression—took form. One part cheesecake emporium, one part gourmet food and wine shop (the old money vault became a wine cellar), and one part caterer, FORM has the feel of an old-fashioned neighborhood grocery. There's even the modern equivalent of a porch where old guys hang out and whittle. Under the drive-through teller awning, now enclosed with netting, stands a ping-pong table that invites customers and neighbors to drop by and play a game—or three.

How did cheesecake get in the mix here? Well, Torres has a passion for them and has spent a lot of time perfecting the basic recipe and developing new flavors, and Kleinschmidt has discovered that he has a particular talent for making them. Since all three partners are ardent champions of local and regional products, FORM features as much local fare as possible, including its own coffee blend from Perc Coffee (see Local Roasted, page

118), fresh pastas from FraLi Gourmet (see Pasta Fresca, page 156), and cheeses from regional dairies like Sweet Grass Dairy in south Georgia. After a soft opening in October 2010 with cheese and gourmet food products, they added wine a month later and have slowly grown a steady clientele for catering, private dinner parties, and special wine-tasting dinners. They've also started a local cheese-of-the-month club that is offered with and without wine.

The spirit of these three gregarious, energetic men can be summed up by the footnote to their business hours posted on the website. The shop closes at seven; however, "if we are there playing ping-pong after hours, *ever* . . . stop on by!"

Smoked Tomato Soup

Courtesy Chef Claude Auerbach

(SERVES 6–8)

You may garnish the soup with sour cream flavored with lime juice or with heavy cream flavored with fresh basil. You can also garnish with chives.

Hickory, peach, or apple wood chips, as needed
(optional; use only if smoking vegetables)

1 onion, peeled and sliced ½ inch thick

2 shallots, peeled and halved lengthwise

12 ripe Roma tomatoes, halved lengthwise

8 tablespoons (1 stick) unsalted butter

⅛ cup dry sherry

1 cup dry white wine

2 bay leaves

3 sprigs thyme

4 cups vegetable or chicken stock

Juice from 1 (8-ounce) can smoked chipotle peppers
(optional; use only if not smoking vegetables)

1 cup half-and-half

Salt and freshly milled black pepper

If you have a smoker, prepare it according to the manufacturer's directions and smoke the onions, shallots, and tomatoes with hickory, peach, or apple wood chips for about 1 hour, or until the smoked flavor and aroma is pronounced. If you don't have a smoker, omit this step and proceed as follows.

Finely dice the onions and shallots and roughly chop the tomatoes. Melt the butter in a large stockpot over medium-low heat and add the onions and shallots. Sweat, tossing often, until translucent. Add the sherry and reduce by half, then add the white wine and reduce by half. Add the tomatoes, bay leaves, thyme, and stock. If you have not smoked the vegetables, add the chipotle liquid for a smoky flavor. Simmer 4 to 6 hours. Puree the soup in batches with a blender and strain, if desired. Return it to the pot. If serving warm, reheat the soup gently and add the half-and-half. Taste and season with salt and pepper as needed. If serving chilled, let the soup cool, cover, and refrigerate thoroughly, and add the half-and-half and season just before serving.

FORM Pernil al Horno

FOURTEEN-HOUR SLOW-ROASTED PUERTO RICAN PORK
COURTESY CHEF BRIAN TORRES

(SERVES 8–10)

One of the most popular products is Chef/Owner Brian Torres's *Pernil al Horno,* whole pork shoulder slow roasted for fourteen hours, a holdover from the restaurant. "When Eos was still open," he says with a wry twist to his mouth, "we had regular customers that would yell at me if we ran out!"

1 bone-in pork butt or shoulder
Sea salt
Cajun seasoning, to taste
Freshly milled black pepper, to taste
Garlic powder, to taste
2 cups red wine
1 cup balsamic vinegar
1 cup soy sauce
Pork or chicken stock

Preheat the oven to 275°F. Using a knife, deeply pierce the pork in at least 12 spots. Place it in a deep roasting pan and rub the surface of the pork with salt, then cover first with Cajun seasoning and then with a layer of black pepper.

Top with a dusting of garlic powder, then add the wine, balsamic vinegar, and enough stock to come about three-quarters of the way up the sides of the pork. Cover the pan tightly with foil and roast 10 to 14 hours, or until fork tender.

GARIBALDI CAFE

315 WEST CONGRESS STREET
(912) 232-7118
WWW.GARIBALDISAVANNAH.COM
OWNERS: DINING GROUP SOUTH
EXECUTIVE CHEF: GERALD GREEN

With its romantic Belle Époque decor, Garibaldi Cafe, located in a restored nineteenth-century firehouse in the old City Market district, calls to mind the historic restaurants of New Orleans's old French Quarter. But this thirty-year-old institution is pure old Savannah, and its decor really harkens back to the glamour of the city's glory days in the late nineteenth century. Its home is the old Germania Fire House, built around 1871 for the German Volunteer Firemen, which has been an integral part of Savannah's dining and community life from its inception. Not merely a volunteer firehouse, Germania House was also an active community center—so active, in fact, that when the city established its own fire departments and eliminated the network of volunteer firemen, the station remained open as a thriving social club, with a saloon on the ground floor and opulent ballroom above.

For the first two decades of Garibaldi's history here, the restaurant occupied only the ground floor, and the handsome upstairs ballroom, its former elegance faded and in bad repair, was unused. But today the room has been lavishly restored to provide additional dining space for the restaurant and allow for private parties and receptions. With its yards of mirrors, tall Palladian window, gilded wrought iron, and lush potted ferns, it provides locals of a certain age with welcome memories of dances past and visitors with a rare glimpse into the glamorous world of Savannah's Victorian era.

The kitchen at Garibaldi is presided over by Chef Gerald Green, a jovial, outgoing man known for his fresh way with local seafood and, in tribute to the restaurant's name, suave interpretations of classic Italian fare. Chef Green's philosophy is pretty straightforward: "I just tell them to use the best ingredients and don't try to take shortcuts." Enough said.

VEAL CHOP AU POIVRE WITH WILD MUSHROOM BRANDY CREAM

(SERVES 4)

A specialty of Garibaldi (and a favorite of Chef Green's) is this peppercorn-crusted veal chop finished with a suave wild mushroom, brandy, and cream sauce.

4 (16-ounce) thick-cut bone-in veal rib chops
¼ cup (about 1 ounce) cracked peppercorns
Salt
2 ounces (four tablespoons) garlic butter (see note)
8 ounces sliced mixed mushrooms
¼ cup brandy
½ cup chicken stock
2 cups heavy cream (40 percent milk fat)
2 tablespoons (¼ stick) unsalted butter, softened
4 cups mashed potatoes, cooked
12 ounces *haricots verts* (green beans), trimmed and cooked al dente in salted water

Prepare the veal chops: Preheat the oven to 375°F. Sprinkle both sides of the veal chops with cracked pepper, pressing gently so that it adheres to the meat, and season lightly with salt. Heat a large ovenproof sauté pan over medium-high heat. Add the garlic butter and let it melt. Add the chops and sear well on both sides. Add the mushrooms to the pan and toss until they are beginning to color. Pour the brandy into the pan and, leaning away, carefully ignite it. When the flame subsides, add the stock and then the cream. Stir and transfer the pan to the oven. Bake

12 minutes, or until the chops are done to your taste (at Garibaldi they are served medium rare).

To serve: Remove the chops to four warmed serving plates. Return the pan to medium-high heat and let it reduce until the sauce is lightly thickened. Finish the sauce with the butter, pour it over the chops, and quickly divide the mashed potatoes and *haricots verts* among the plates. Serve immediately.

Note: To make the garlic butter, allow 1½ ounces (about 2 large cloves) fresh garlic for every 8 tablespoons softened butter. Peel and put the garlic through a garlic press and then scrape it to a puree with the edge of a knife. Combine it with the butter and mix well. Transfer the garlic butter to a covered storage container and refrigerate until needed.

Linguine with Clams in Garlic Cream Garibaldi

(SERVES 4)

About 60 live littleneck clams

1½ cups dry white wine

1½ cups water

Juice of about 1 lemon

1¾ cups heavy cream (40 percent milk fat)

½ cup freshly grated Parmigiano Reggiano

Whole black pepper in a mill

Salt

¾ pound linguine

6 tablespoons garlic butter (see note to preceding recipe on page 81)

Chopped parsley

Bring 4 quarts water to a rolling boil for linguine.

Scrub the clams under cold running water and let them drain. Bring the wine, water, and lemon juice to taste to a boil in a large, heavy-bottomed stockpot or dutch oven. Let it boil until it is slightly reduced and the wine loses its sharp, alcoholic smell. Add the clams, cover, and steam just until they open. Lift out the clams and set them aside in a bowl. Add the cream, bring it to a boil, and let it cook until slightly thickened. Stir in the Parmigiano and season with pepper to taste. Do not add salt: The clams will be very salty already. Turn off the heat and put the clams back in the sauce.

Lightly salt the boiling water and stir in the linguine. Cook, stirring occasionally, until it is al dente. Drain and add it to the clam sauce. Return the pan to the heat and reheat briefly. Add the garlic butter and toss until it has just melted and thickened the sauce. Sprinkle with parsley and serve immediately.

Green Truck Neighborhood Pub

2430 Habersham Street
(912) 234-5885
www.greentruckpub.com
Owner: Joshua Yates

Over the last two decades, the old, settled, and often segregated neighborhoods of Savannah's Midtown have been undergoing a transition. The sharply drawn borders have blurred and started to run together, creating a lively mix of multiple ethnic groups, students and professionals, young families and retirees. This melting-pot blend has made for fertile ground in which some of Savannah's most interesting neighborhood cafes, restaurants, and pubs have sprouted.

A prime example of the trend is Green Truck Neighborhood Pub, a thriving hot spot in the unlikely location of a converted 1970s fast-food joint. Its rust-colored walls decorated with vintage hubcaps and a handful of other antique automobile artifacts, its cast-concrete bar lit by fixtures that owner Josh Yates made himself from vintage Mason canning jars, this lively little place is exactly what he set out to create: the American version of the neighborhood pubs found in virtually every village throughout the British Isles.

Yates's original concept for the menu, in fact, was to offer the kind of food traditionally served in those pubs—fish–and–chips, shepherd's pie, and the like. But once he settled on the location, the menu organically grew into something more solidly American—sandwiches, salads, soups, chili, and, of course, that most American of pub foods, hamburgers. Made from locally raised grass-fed beef and offered with an array of toppings from all-American lettuce and tomato to goat cheese and balsamic-caramelized onions, the burgers have become Green Truck's signature dish.

The philosophy behind the food can be summed up by the manifesto printed on the back of the menu: "Some say nothing worth doing is ever easy, and we think easy food is rarely worth eating. Which is why we do simple food the hard way: from scratch."

They're not kidding around. Almost everything served here, including the ketchup and pickles, is made in house. Yates also believes in supporting other local businesses, and below that manifesto is a proud list of the local vendors who supply their beef, coffee, poultry, pork, tofu, and produce. A former manufacturing engineer, he explains, "Over the years, I lost respect for packaged, manufactured foods. I came to this from a factory—so I know what they're like."

Green Truck has only been open since October 2010, but to Yates and his loyal regulars, for whom the place has become an indispensable part of the neighborhood, it seems a lot longer. He smiles and sighs, "Yeah, around here we call them 'Green Truck' years; they're like dog years."

GREEN TRUCK PIMIENTO CHEESE

(MAKES ABOUT 5 CUPS)

A signature of the pub is the house-made pimiento cheese. Used mainly for sandwiches, either atop the popular Trailer Park burger or slathered on toasted bread with lettuce and tomato (ask them to add crisp bacon to send it over the top), it's also offered as an appetizer spread, plated with house-made pickles and crostini. At home, you might also try slathering it onto celery sticks or dropping a heaped spoonful into a split hot baked potato.

1 (4-ounce) jar diced pimientos
1 cup mayonnaise
1 clove garlic, minced
1 tablespoon freshly squeezed lemon juice
1 teaspoon dry mustard (Coleman's preferred)
¼ teaspoon ground cayenne pepper
1 pound sharp cheddar, shredded (see note)

Thoroughly drain the pimientos, gently pressing them to remove as much moisture as possible (this prevents the whole thing turning pink). In a glass or nonreactive stainless steel mixing bowl, gently combine them with the remaining ingredients, taking care not to overwork the cheese.

Note: It's important to use good cheese and shred it yourself with a coarse grater, since packaged preshredded cheese is often coated with starch or wax to keep it from clumping, and that coating will adversely affect the texture and flavor.

Green Truck Georgia Spiced Nuts

(MAKES 3 CUPS)

Another signature nibble at Green Truck is local pecans and walnuts, toasted with an addictive rosemary-scented butter-and-caramel glaze.

1½ cups local pecan halves

1½ cups walnut halves

3½ tablespoons unsalted butter

2½ tablespoons light brown sugar

1 teaspoon ground cayenne pepper

2 tablespoons finely minced fresh rosemary

About 1½ teaspoons coarse kosher salt, to taste

Preheat the oven to 375°F. Arrange the pecans and walnuts on a rimmed baking sheet in a single layer and toast just until hot through and fragrant, about 3 to 4 minutes in a convection oven or 7 to 8 minutes in a conventional oven.

Meanwhile, melt the butter and brown sugar in a small saucepan over medium heat. Remove it from the heat and mix in the cayenne, rosemary, and salt (to taste). Remove the nuts from the oven and pour them into a large mixing bowl, immediately pour the butter mixture over them, and toss until they are evenly and completely coated. The nuts must be hot or the butter mixture won't adhere to them. Pour them back onto the baking sheet, spread them out to separate them, and bake 3 to 5 minutes longer in a convection oven or about 8 minutes in a conventional one. Let the nuts cool completely on the pan before transferring them to a lidded storage container.

HUNTER CATTLE COMPANY

430 Driggers Road
Brooklet, Georgia 30415
(912) 823-2333
www.huntercattle.com
Owners: Del and Debra Ferguson

Located just west of Savannah in the little farming community of Brooklet, Hunter Cattle Company is a family farm owned and operated by Del and Debra Ferguson, a warmhearted pair of self-described "plain old country folks." Specializing primarily in pasture-raised cattle, this animal welfare–certified farm also naturally raises heirloom breeds of hogs and poultry, and will soon add sheep to the menagerie. The Fergusons have become major vendors for the growing number of community-conscious restaurateurs like Green Truck Neighborhood Pub (page 83) owner Josh Yates, who says that they treat their growing circle of customers like family. As a matter of fact, on the Pub's first anniversary, Yates celebrated by renting a church bus to take his staff out to the farm for a daylong outing.

Jazz'd Tapas Bar

52 Barnard Street
(912) 236-7777
www.jazzdsavannah.com
Owners: Brian and Julie Curry
Executive Chef: Brian Gonet

Stepping from the sidewalk onto the steps that lead down to Jazz'd Tapas Bar feels a little bit like stepping onto a stairway through time—back to one of those clandestine speakeasies from the Prohibition era of the 1920s. That sense of time travel ends, however, at the threshold. This youthful nightspot may be below street level, but there is nothing clandestine or retro about the sleek, ultramodern black-and-red decor. Called "one of the sexiest places in the world" by no less than *Cosmopolitan* magazine, its young, urban-hip crowd, fusion tapas menu, and nightly changing, bluesy live music give Jazz'd the kind of cutting-edge atmosphere usually found in much larger cities.

An urbane collection of tapas-size plates that is as suave as the decor, the menu at Jazz'd is fusion in the best sense of the word. Rather than a confused jumble of cuisines on a single plate, each dish is pretty straightforward and simple; it's the menu that cross-sections the world's cuisines with a truly international blend from Central America to Southeast Asia to the traditional cookery found right here in Savannah. The tapas concept was the main attraction for Executive Chef Brian Gonet, in part because it afforded him the freedom to explore many different cuisines, and in part because it fit the trend he was seeing among patrons for more reasonable portions.

He's noticed that people nowadays are looking for smaller plates instead of huge entrees, and likes that lighter (and less expensive) portions afford diners the freedom to taste several different things at one meal and yet still keep the cost of that meal within their budget. His concept for the food on those small plates is to keep it simple and clean, saying that he prefers to let each thing speak for itself instead of covering it up with layers of different flavors just for the sake of novelty.

The plates may be simple, but the menu offers a broad range of flavors, everything from a traditional French onion soup enlivened with five kinds of onions, to beef kebabs seasoned with a Cuban-style rub, to such Thai-accented offerings as local shrimp encrusted with coconut, to finger-food chicken salad with a Thai accent, in which lettuce fills in for a flatbread or rice-paper wrapper.

Chicken Lettuce Wrap with Peanut Curry Sauce

(SERVES 6–8)

For the sauce:

1 (14-ounce) can coconut milk

2 tablespoons red curry paste (available at Asian grocers)

2 tablespoons creamy peanut butter

Pinch of ground cayenne pepper

¼ cup water

3 tablespoons cornstarch

For the chicken:

10 cloves garlic, peeled and chopped

2 tablespoons crushed red pepper flakes

1½ cups teriyaki sauce

½ cup plus 3 tablespoons extra-virgin olive oil

2½ pounds boneless, skinless chicken breast

2 leeks, washed and thinly sliced into rings

2 red bell peppers, cored, seeded, and cut into strips

½ cup dry-roasted, unsalted peanuts

3 jalapeño peppers, cored and cut into strips

2 heads romaine lettuce, divided into leaves and washed

¼ head red cabbage, shredded

3 carrots, peeled and shredded

2 red onions, trimmed, peeled, and thinly sliced

Make the sauce: Combine the coconut milk, curry paste, peanut butter, and cayenne in a 2-quart saucepan and bring it a boil. Whisk together the water and cornstarch until completely dissolved. Slowly whisk the cornstarch solution into the sauce and cook, whisking constantly, until thickened. Turn off the heat and let the mixture cool. The sauce can be made ahead, cooled, and refrigerated, but let it sit at room temperature for at least 30 minutes before serving.

Make the chicken: In a glass or nonreactive stainless steel bowl, combine the garlic, pepper flakes, teriyaki, and ½ cup olive oil. Add the chicken and gently toss to coat. Cover and refrigerate overnight.

Remove the chicken from the refrigerator and let it sit at room temperature for 30 minutes. Prepare a grill (or use a stovetop grill pan) for a medium-hot fire. Grill the chicken, turning once, until cooked through, about 4 to 5 minutes per side. Let rest 10 minutes, slice into strips, and set aside.

Heat the remaining 3 tablespoons olive oil in a large skillet over medium-high heat. Add the leeks, bell pepper, peanuts, and jalapeños, and sauté 2 minutes, tossing regularly. Add the chicken and the teriyaki mixture and cook until the liquid is completely absorbed. Serve with lettuce leaves, cabbage, shredded carrots, red onions, and sauce, letting diners build their own wraps.

THE HIPPIE GROCERS

Brighter Day Natural Foods
1102 Bull Street (Entrance on Park Avenue)
(912) 236-4703
Owners: Peter and Janie Brodhead

When Peter and Janie Brodhead, Savannah's self-described "hippie grocers," first opened their natural food store on the south end of Forsyth Park in 1978, everyone said they had lost their minds, that there was no market in this old, set-in-its-ways city for herbal remedies and "nuts and bark" hippie food. Moreover, the surrounding Victorian District neighborhood was just catching the restoration bug and was, to put it politely, a bit dicey. But the Brodheads just smiled and kept going—and proved everyone wrong. The first—and for years only—grocer to offer an extensive and comprehensive stock of organic foods, Brighter Day was also an early supporter of the handful of local farmers who were trying to bring back natural agriculture. Now a downtown institution, it has expanded from a tiny corner shop to a thriving market at the forefront of the city's locavore movement. When it first opened, the organic produce in its bins and dairy products in its coolers were mostly trucked in. There was only the occasional basket of locally grown produce. Today, they are supplied by an extensive network of local and regional vendors, including Southern Swiss Dairy (see Dairy to the [Culinary] Stars, page 75), a local dairy offering organic, non-homogenized dairy products.

The Lady & Sons

102 West Congress Street
(912) 233-2600
Owners: Paula, Jamie, and Bobby Deen

Surely no one needs an introduction to the restaurant with bright red-and-white striped awnings sitting in the middle of Savannah's historic downtown on the corner of Congress and Whitaker Streets. Nor do they need an introduction to its owners, colorful television cooking celebrity Paula Deen and her sons Jamie and Bobby Deen. By now everyone knows the story of how a woman crippled by agoraphobia managed to conquer her demons and spin a door-to-door bagged-lunch service and signature "y'all" into a Southern cooking empire.

Few realize, however, that Paula Deen's rise from that modest cottage industry in her home kitchen was neither as facile nor meteoric as it might seem from the outside. Though The Bag Lady's wholesome, homemade lunches were an immediate success with downtown office workers, the business's growth was slow. First it graduated to a commercial kitchen in the empty restaurant of a Southside motel. Later, the Deens began offering a Southern-style buffet lunch in the unused dining room. But only after Paula and her sons were comfortable with the dining room's success did they contemplate moving the restaurant downtown to City Market. And at every step of the way, all three struggled with whether or not they wanted to work this hard for the rest of their lives.

For several years, The Lady & Sons enjoyed modest success in a City Market storefront just a few blocks from the present location. Aided by a close-knit group of employees, it served up mountains of perfect fried chicken; fresh, simply cooked Southern-style vegetables; cheese biscuits; and hoecakes to locals and visitors. Paula remained a constant presence in those years; locals knew that when she wasn't out in the dining room, they could find her in the kitchen at the fryer, covered in flour and dropping breaded chicken into boiling fat.

Then came television and fame—and everything changed. Before long, the little restaurant was overwhelmed, forcing the

Deens to cast around for other options. They ended up settling on the present location, the former home of White Hardware, an old downtown institution that had closed several years before. With three stories of dining rooms, a full-service bar, and a network of serving stations, they thought they were set. They were wrong. The restaurant continues to draw visitors by the thousands, and the challenge today is how to maintain the quality that made this restaurant legendary without turning anyone away—because that, y'all, is a lot of fried chicken.

The Lady & Sons Chicken Pot Pie

(SERVES 4)

4 sheets frozen puff pastry

1 egg, beaten

4 chicken breast halves, or 2 cups leftover cooked chicken

Paula Deen Seasoned Salt

Freshly milled black pepper

2 tablespoons cooking oil

⅓ cup melted unsalted butter

⅔ cup flour

1 quart heavy cream

¼ cup chicken broth base, available in most supermarkets

1 tablespoon minced garlic

½ small yellow onion, minced

1 cup frozen green peas, cooked

1 cup cooked carrots, chopped

Pinch fresh grated nutmeg (optional)

Preheat the oven to 350°F. Choose four individual pot pie dishes, ramekins, or gratin dishes that will hold at least 20 ounces (2½ cups). Cut each sheet of frozen puff pastry into strips 1 inch wide and 8 inches long. On a large cookie sheet, weave the strips into a lattice large enough to cover each pot pie. Beat the egg and brush onto each lattice square. Bake for 5 minutes. Dough will rise and turn light golden brown. Set aside until ready to assemble pies. Do not turn off the oven.

If using cooked leftover chicken, skip to the next step. Season the chicken breasts with seasoned salt and pepper to taste. Heat 2 tablespoons oil in a skillet and sauté the chicken breasts until cooked through, about 4 minutes per side. Cut into chunks and set aside.

In a large saucepan melt the butter and slowly add the flour, stirring until it is the consistency of peanut butter but not browned. Slowly stir in the cream and keep stirring. Add the chicken base, garlic, and onion, and stir until thickened. Add the peas, carrots, nutmeg (if using), and chicken, and remove the pan from heat.

Divide the filling among four ovenproof bowls, filling them completely. Top each with one of the precooked lattice squares.

Bake in the preheated oven for 5 minutes or until bubbly. If there is any remaining pie filling, it can be frozen for later use.

Leoci's Trattoria

606 Abercorn Street
(912) 335-7027
www.leocis.com
Owner/Executive Chef: Roberto Leoci
Co-Owner: Lacie Leoci

Chef Roberto Leoci was born in Canada, but his roots—and his heart, soul, and palate—are firmly planted in Italy. His passion for food was awakened at his Italian parents' table, where the food became a touchstone to home, and was nurtured by annual summer-long visits to his family in Sicily.

After finishing his basic college education on this side of the pond, he returned to Italy to study cooking in Florence, both formally in a cooking school and as an apprentice in local restaurants. His career began at the Ritz-Carleton in Key Biscayne and followed a fairly conventional path, until the fateful day he was asked to help a friend open a restaurant in the heart of Savannah's historic downtown. Falling hard for the old town, Leoci was soon looking for a way to stay after his contract was finished and share his passion for Italian food with his new love.

He found that way at 606 Abercorn, a late Victorian building with a funky 1950s face and a long history in Savannah's food community. After updating the kitchen, adding a dining deck on the back of the building, and giving the dining room a stylish urban-Italian makeover, he and wife Lacie opened Leoci's Trattoria in late 2009. With a solid menu of back-to-basics Italian cuisine, Leoci is committed to authentic regional cookery, but with an emphasis on fresh, local, and seasonal ingredients. His house-made pastas, brick-oven bread and pizzas, authentic risotti, and classic entrees all remain true to the spirit of Italian cooking, but tap into a wealth of local ingredients.

That commitment to quality local products has recently led Leoci into a partnership with Hunter Cattle Company (see sidebar, page 85), a nearby rancher who produces pastured grass-fed beef and heirloom pork. Following Leoci's recipes and natural curing methods, Hunter is now producing traditionally cured meats and sausages for the restaurant.

Orecchiette Bari-Bari

(SERVES 6)

An especially popular specialty of the house that incorporates the sausage is this simple dish of orecchiette (or "little ears"), little rounds of fresh egg pasta hand-shaped into an ear-like cup, hence the name. Here they are sauced with a mild house-made link sausage and fresh broccolini.

For the fresh orecchiette pasta (makes about 1 pound):

1 pound plus 1 ounce semolina flour
4 large eggs
2 large egg yolks
Water, as needed
Salt, for cooking

5 small links mild Italian sausage (Leoci uses a
   house-made pork sausage)
2 tablespoons olive oil
2 cloves garlic, lightly crushed, peeled, and minced
2 heads broccolini, washed and cut into bite-size pieces
1 pound cooked fresh orecchiette pasta
2 cups chicken stock
5 sprigs fresh sage, chopped
6 tablespoons unsalted butter, cut into small chunks

Parmigiano Reggiano cheese, for serving

Make the pasta: Mound the flour on a wooden or plastic-laminated work surface. Put the eggs and yolks in a mixing bowl and lightly beat them together. Make a well in the center of the flour and pour in the eggs. Using a fork, gradually mix the flour into the eggs until it clumps together and forms a firm dough, adding a small amount of cool water as needed to make the dough smooth.

Knead the pasta until it is very smooth, about 7 to 8 minutes. Cut it into several pieces and roll each piece out into a cylinder about 1-inch thick. Wrap with plastic wrap and refrigerate until firm.

To shape the pasta, keep the dough chilled until you are ready to shape it. Unwrap 1 piece and thinly slice it. With floured hands, quickly take each slice, put it into your hand, and press with the thumb of the other hand to form a little ear-shaped cup. Continue with the remaining pasta until it is all shaped.

Bring 4 quarts water to a boil. Add a handful of salt, stir, and then stir in the orecchiette. Cook until al dente and drain.

To prepare the dish: Slice the sausage on the diagonal into bite-size pieces. Put the oil and sausage in a large sauté pan that will hold all the ingredients at once. Turn on the heat to medium high and sauté until the sausage is lightly browned. Add the garlic and toss until fragrant. Add the broccolini and toss until bright green. Add the orecchiette and toss.

Add the chicken stock, sage, and butter, and toss until the butter is melted into a velvety sauce. Serve immediately, passing freshly grated Parmigiano Reggiano separately, if desired.

LEOPOLD'S ICE CREAM

212 EAST BROUGHTON STREET
(912) 234-4442
WWW.LEOPOLDSICECREAM.COM
OWNERS: STRATTON AND MARY LEOPOLD

In a place so rich with history that virtually every crack in the sidewalk is a protected monument, it says something for Leopold's Ice Cream that the mere mention of its name stirs deeper sighs of nostalgia for native Savannahians than any of its grand architectural monuments.

Founded in 1919 by Greek immigrant brothers George, Basil, and Peter Leopold, the original Leopold's was located at the intersection of Gwinnett and Habersham Streets, just a block away from the birthplace of famed songwriter Johnny Mercer. Mercer grew up on Leopold's ice cream, and was so in love with their signature Tutti-Frutti that he vowed that someday he'd write a song about it. While he never got around to it (probably too busy licking a cone of the stuff), his passion for it became nearly as legendary as the ice cream itself.

By the time Peter Leopold's son Stratton took over the business, however, the neighborhood surrounding it had changed, and it was no longer a viable location. Stratton made the hard decision to close and pursue a successful career producing films. But he carefully preserved the recipes and many of the original fixtures, and after being badgered for years by his childhood friends, he and his wife, Mary, finally found the right location on recently revitalized Broughton Street and reopened.

Fitted with so many of the original fixtures (including a wood-paneled phone booth), its freezer cases filled with ice creams made in-house, exactly as they had been in its heyday, the new Leopold's is, for Savannahians of a certain age, a welcome blast back to their childhood; for youngsters, it's a glimpse of an old Savannah they never knew.

Stratton and Mary have fed that nostalgia by gradually bringing back many of the old specialties but, not content to rest on Leopold's old laurels, are always experimenting with new flavors. Joining the tutti-frutti that inspired Johnny Mercer are seasonal offerings like cinnamon, rose petal, and lavender.

OLIVE & CREAM CHEESE SANDWICH

(MAKES ABOUT 1½ CUPS, OR 4–6 SANDWICHES)

Well, those legendary ice cream recipes are family secrets, and are likely to remain so. But another Leopold's classic that has been on the menu since 1919 is the olive and cream cheese sandwich. This simple spread of cream cheese studded with chopped stuffed olives has entered the Savannah culinary lexicon, and to this day is a fixture at church receptions and cocktail parties all over town. It's served on warm whole wheat toast in the cafe but can be used in any way that you'd use pimiento cheese—on plain white bread for a cold sandwich, as a cocktail spread with crackers, on crostini or warm bruschetta, or piped into fresh celery sticks.

Try grilling it until the bread is crisp and the filling, warm, gooey, and luscious.

8 ounces cream cheese
⅓ cup chopped pimiento-stuffed Spanish olives
Olive pickling juice, as needed
Sliced whole grain sandwich bread

Put the cream cheese into a mixing bowl and let it soften to room temperature. Add the olives and mix them in. Mix in olive pickling juice to taste until the cheese is has a smooth spreading consistency. The spread will keep, covered and refrigerated, for up to two weeks.

To make the sandwich as served at Leopold's, toast two slices of the best whole grain bread you can get. While it is still quite warm, slather one piece of bread generously with the cream cheese and olive spread, top with the second slice, and serve immediately.

LOCAL 11TEN

1110 BULL STREET
(912) 790-9000
WWW.LOCAL11TEN.COM
EXECUTIVE CHEF: BRANDY WILLIAMSON

Outside Local 11Ten, you're on a sidewalk in Savannah's Victorian District neighborhood, but the moment you step over the threshold of its sleek, polished stainless steel door you feel as if you've crossed a timeline into a stylish Manhattan dining room. Formerly a bank in the south end of the historic Veterans of Foreign Wars building, the restaurant's decor, in contrast to its yellow brick and cast stone Tudor-Gothic exterior, is sleek and contemporary, and its staff is made up of smart, urban-chic young people. But that is where the resemblance to New York ends. Appropriately just around the corner from Brighter Day (see The Hippie Grocers, page 89), the venerable natural foods grocery that lit the spark for Savannah's locavore culture more than thirty years ago, and steps away from the site of downtown's Saturday farmers' market (see Market Fresh, page 101), this restaurant has "local" in its name for a reason. While the cuisine is as contemporary as the dining room's decor, it is deeply rooted in traditional Southern foodways, with a conscious emphasis on locally produced meat, poultry, vegetables, fruits, and dairy products, wild-caught local seafood, regional cheeses and cured meats, right down to their own blend of coffee locally roasted by Perc Coffee (see Local Roasted, page 118).

Keeping the kitchen true to that vision is Executive Chef Brandy Williamson, a quietly passionate native Southerner who credits her belief in cooking and eating local to her upbringing in a small town in rural North Carolina. She explains, "I was raised cooking with my mom from the time I could walk. By the time I was twelve, I was out hunting with my dad in the morning, and by evening was in the kitchen with mom, cooking what we'd bagged—so I really understand the eating local concept on a gut level."

She went on to study cooking in France and trained at Le Cordon Bleu, and describes her style as "simple Southern food given a refined edge from my French training. If I have a philosophy, it's that I believe food in its simplest form is best for the mind and the body.

"It just makes sense to cook and eat locally," she shrugs as if this was obvious. To that end, the menu changes seasonally, and descriptions often remain somewhat open-ended, allowing for changes to accommodate produce that's locally available that day. The roasted root vegetables that accompany the grilled pork chop, for example, can be whatever happens to be fresh in your own market.

Apricot Glazed Grilled Pork Loin Chops with Garlic Roasted Root Vegetables, Broccolini & Chimichurri Cream

(SERVES 4)

For the apricot jam glaze (makes about 3 cups):

6 ounces dried apricots, chopped
3 cups water
1½ cups sugar
1 tablespoon freshly squeezed lemon juice

For the chimichurri cream (makes about 1¾ cups):

1 cup firmly packed parsley leaves
2 tablespoons chopped fresh oregano
2 tablespoons chopped fresh cilantro
½ jalapeño pepper, seeded and roughly chopped
4 cloves garlic, crushed, peeled, and roughly chopped
1 shallot, peeled and roughly chopped
Freshly squeezed juice of 1 lime
2 tablespoons red wine vinegar
⅓ cup olive oil
¼ cup white wine
1 tablespoon minced shallot
1 sprig fresh thyme
¼ cup heavy cream
½ pound cold butter, cut into cubes
Salt and freshly milled black pepper, to taste

For the roasted root vegetables:

Salt
2 pounds assorted root vegetables, washed and trimmed
2 cloves garlic, minced
2 tablespoons chopped assorted fresh herbs
Olive oil

For the broccolini and pork:

Salt
2 pounds broccolini, stems trimmed
Olive oil
Freshly milled black pepper
4 (12-ounce) bone-in pork loin chops
Melted butter (optional)

To make the jam glaze: Combine the apricots, water, sugar, and lemon juice in a plastic container, cover, and let sit overnight at room temperature.

Transfer the mixture to a heavy-bottomed enamel-lined or stainless steel saucepan and simmer over medium heat until reduced to syrupy consistency. Turn off the heat and let cool.

To make the chimichurri cream: Combine the parsley, oregano, cilantro, jalapeño, garlic, and shallot in a blender. Add the lime juice and vinegar and turn on the machine. Slowly add the oil in a thin, steady stream until blended.

Combine the wine, shallot, and thyme in an enamel- or stainless steel–lined saucepan and reduce until almost dry. Add the cream and reduce by half. Add ½ cup chimichurri and bring it to a simmer. Remove it from the heat and quickly whisk in the butter in bits until incorporated. Season with salt and pepper as needed. Hold over hot (not simmering) water until needed.

To prepare the roasted root vegetables: Prepare a large basin of ice and water. Bring a large pot of water to a boil and salt it well. Add the root vegetables and cook until just tender (not mushy). Remove them from the boiling water and drop them into the ice water bath. When cooled,

drain and pat dry. Shortly before serving, preheat the oven to 350°F and toss the vegetables in a bowl with the garlic, herbs, and oil. Spread them on a rimmed sheet pan and roast about 5 minutes, or until hot. Keep warm.

To prepare the broccolini: If necessary, replenish the basin of ice water with ice. Bring a large pot of water to a boil and salt it well. Add the broccolini and cook 1 minute. Drain and drop into the ice water bath. When cooled, drain and pat dry. Shortly before serving, toss the broccolini in a bowl with olive oil, salt, and pepper. While the chops are grilling, grill the broccolini for about 2 to 3 minutes, turning occasionally. Keep warm.

To prepare the chops: Prepare a grill with a medium hot fire. Rub the chops with butter (or olive oil, if preferred) and season both sides with salt and pepper. Grill 5 to 6 minutes per side or until the desired internal temperature is reached (Local 11Ten serves the chops medium—about 145° F). Remove from the heat and let rest 3 minutes before serving.

To serve: Ready four warm serving plates. Place 3 or 4 of each vegetable on each plate, position a chop next to the vegetables, and spread some of the apricot glaze over it. Drizzle the chimichurri cream around the plate and serve immediately.

MARKET FRESH

Forsyth Farmers' Market
Forsyth Park at Park Avenue
www.forsythfarmersmarket.org

Every Saturday morning from early spring until late autumn, downtowners in Savannah have been rediscovering the pleasures of shopping for truly fresh-from-the-farm food for the first time since the old market building on Ellis Square was demolished in 1955. While still modest compared to more established markets in larger cities, it has put down solid roots and is lively, vibrant, and growing steadily.

From its beginnings in 2009, when a handful of brave vendors set up on the very end of the park's south promenade, it has expanded to more than thirty. It nearly fills both sides of the promenade from Park Avenue all the way to the Confederate Monument at the park's midpoint and offers everything from fresh local produce to grass-fed meat, free-range poultry, first-quality dairy products, local honey, baked goods, and coffee, as well as potted plants, seeds, and seedlings for home gardeners.

Because the vendors grow or make everything that they sell, they not only have a vested commitment to their products, they've a wealth of knowledge about them and are never too busy to pause and swap recipes or advise customers on taking care of and preparing an unfamiliar vegetable or pasture-raised meat. In other words, they don't just stop at selling it; they want to make sure that you get the most from it after you've taken it home to the kitchen. Consequently, the best way to shop this (or any other) farmers' market is to go without a set plan, keeping your eyes and mind open to what you find, instead of what you've decided you want to find.

Lulu's Chocolate Bar

42 Martin Luther King Jr. Boulevard
(912) 238-2012, (866) 461-8681
www.luluschocolatebar.net
Owners: Rebecca Freeman and Janine Finn

Bars that serve food are nothing new: Fast, easy, thirst-creating nibbles have been a staple of taverns since time immemorial. A dessert cafe that serves cocktails, however, is not something one stumbles upon every day. Yet that is exactly what you'll find in Lulu's Chocolate Bar, a unique little nightspot just around the corner from Broughton Street on up-and-coming MLK Boulevard. Though primarily a dessert cafe, beyond the sumptuous display of desserts in the glass case at the front door is a full-service bar, offering everything from espresso to signature dessert cocktails to a drinking chocolate that is like sipping a melted truffle. While that may seem an unlikely combination, for owners Rebecca Freeman and Janine Finn, it has been a formula for success.

For years these two friends had talked about opening a business together. But while Rebecca had been catering and baking desserts for local restaurants for several years, neither of them had any real experience in running a food-service-type business and never really imagined that they could own a restaurant of their own. And anyway, they'd never arrived at a business concept that really sparkled for them. But then Janine happened onto a late-night dessert cafe while visiting Asheville, North Carolina, and was immediately taken by it. When she shared the idea with Rebecca, they both knew they'd found the business they'd been looking for.

Rebecca explains that the business that inspired them was not a bar, but truly a dessert cafe, serving only coffee and sweets; the bar concept for Lulu's was really an afterthought. "We just thought—well, it's Savannah, so we'd better have a bar."

But then they started to explore all the dessert cocktails that were making news in other trendy nightspots, and Janine brought in sipping chocolate, which she'd had in Spain. Suddenly, the bar became a natural extension of the dessert menu and began to make perfect sense.

The desserts are Rebecca's creations. She'd loved baking for as long as she could remember, and though you wouldn't know it by looking at her slim figure, she has a raging sweet tooth. It's a trait she says she inherited from her grandmother, who was the real baker in the family. She explains, "My mother was a good baker, too, but my grandmother was an amazing baker—and a chocoholic!"

This being Savannah, it seems appropriate to begin with Lulu's own version of the famous Bellini. Inspired by the Champagne cocktails and punches that have been mainstays of this city's entertaining for more than two centuries, Lulu's Bellini is revved up with a shot each of premium single-barrel bourbon and peach liqueur.

Savannah Bourbon Bellini

(SERVES 1)

1 ounce Woodford Reserve Bourbon

1 ounce Stirrings Peach Liqueur

3 ounces chilled Spanish Cava or other
   dry sparkling wine

1 ripe peach slice

Stir together the bourbon and peach liqueur, and slowly add the sparkling wine. Put several pieces of ice into a large white wine glass and carefully pour in the cocktail. Garnish the glass with a slice of ripe peach and serve immediately.

Jameson Walnut Tart

(MAKES 1 9-INCH TART, SERVING 6)

Rebecca is always creating, and bar stock frequently finds its way into the desserts, like the Irish whiskey in this sumptuous walnut tart.

For the crust:

½ cup (1 stick) unsalted butter, melted

¼ cup sugar

⅛ teaspoon salt

¾ teaspoon vanilla

1 cup all-purpose flour

For the caramel layer:

⅓ cup water

¾ cup sugar

1 teaspoon corn syrup

2 teaspoons unsalted butter

⅓ cup heavy whipping cream

For the filling:

1 cup chopped walnuts

½ cup chopped dark chocolate

¾ cup light corn syrup

½ cup light brown sugar

½ cup dark brown sugar

4 tablespoons (½ stick) unsalted butter, cut up

3 large eggs

3 tablespoons Jameson Irish Whiskey

1 teaspoon vanilla

½ teaspoon salt

Special Equipment: **fluted 9-inch tart pan, pastry brush**

To make the crust: Preheat the oven to 350°F. Mix together the melted butter, sugar, salt, and vanilla. Add the flour and stir until blended. Press into a fluted 9-inch tart pan. Bake 15 minutes or until just starting to turn golden. Remove it from the oven and let cool.

To make the caramel layer: Combine the water, sugar, and corn syrup in a saucepan over medium-low heat. Swirl occasionally until sugar is dissolved. Increase the heat to medium and cook until sugar is a deep golden-amber color, brushing down the sides of the pan with a pastry brush dipped in water as necessary to keep the caramel from crystallizing. Immediately add the butter and whisk until smooth, then whisk in the cream slowly and carefully as it will bubble vigorously. Pour the caramel into the prepared tart crust and refrigerate until the caramel is set.

To finish the tart: Sprinkle half the walnuts and all the chocolate into the crust on top of the caramel. Combine the corn syrup, both sugars, butter, eggs, whiskey, vanilla, and salt and whisk until smooth and glossy. Pour the mixture carefully into crust and top with the remaining walnuts. Bake in the preheated 350°F oven for 45 to 50 minutes or until nearly set in the center when jiggled.

Magnolia Bakery Cafe

703 Congress Street
Beaufort, SC
(843) 524-1961
www.magnoliacafebeaufort.com
Chefs/Owners: Jing and Dana Johnsrude

On the bustling Congress Street in Beaufort, South Carolina, one of the most picturesque places in all of the Carolina Lowcountry (see the Old Sheldon Church to the left and Historic Beaufort, page 112), the entrance to Magnolia Bakery Cafe stands out. Invitingly shaded by a columned trellis covered in Confederate star jasmine, it lures passersby in almost as effectively as the sweet aroma of baked goods that escapes from its kitchen. Inside, the long, narrow dining room with its pale-blue beaded-board ceiling, wide, full-length windows with an unobstructed view of the waterfront, and sunny, Provençal decor, is a conscientious cross between a cafe somewhere in southern France and the screened living porch of a down-south lake cabin. It's exactly what you'd expect of a place whose menu seamlessly blends French country cooking and baking with Lowcountry seafood and Southern-style sweets. The mix is the natural result of Chef Dana Johnsrude's childhood in North Carolina and formal training in French cooking that included kitchen apprenticeships in and around the Washington area, where the couple lived for many years, and where, as he put it, he was "knocked around by a lot of French chefs."

After working for several years in that high-pressure environment, however, the Johnsrudes began to tire of the hectic schedule and started looking for a place where they could slow the pace and actually have a life outside their business. They wanted to be back in the South, and got in touch with a broker that they happened to know in Charleston. In 2002, they came down for a visit and the broker introduced them to Beaufort. Falling in love with the area, they found out that the Magnolia Bakery Cafe was for sale and bought it almost sight unseen. They've never looked back. As Dana explains, "With a lunch cafe, you get to keep almost banker's hours. Plus, my wife and I had never worked together, and we felt that this was something we could both handle."

The division of responsibilities fell into place organically. While both are classically trained, Dana presides over the kitchen and handles the day-to-day cooking, while Jing manages the front of house and does most of the baking. All the same, there are no sharp divisions of labor here; lately Jing has been spending more time in the kitchen, and Dana has put his hand to some of the baking.

One of the signature specialties of both the breakfast and lunch menu is classic French crepes. There's everything from a Tex-Mex, burrito-style breakfast crepe of sausage, eggs, and salsa, to savory luncheon and sweet dessert crepes. The most popular is stuffed with local blue crab, a filling that Dana created on the spot for a customer. It was an instant hit and has been the star of the menu ever since. That's the one secret he says he'll never part with, but he's happy to share another that is almost as popular, filled with herbed chicken and topped with Mornay sauce.

MAGNOLIA'S CHICKEN HERB CREPES
(SERVES 4)

For the crepes:

½ cup all-purpose flour

1 egg

¼ cup milk

¼ cup water

Pinch of salt

1 tablespoon melted butter

Vegetable oil, for cooking the crepes

For the Mornay sauce:

3 tablespoons unsalted butter

3 tablespoons all-purpose flour

2 cups whole milk, plus additional for thinning
   the sauce (optional)

¼ teaspoon salt

Freshly milled white pepper

Freshly grated nutmeg

1 ounce grated gruyère cheese

1 ounce grated Parmesan cheese

For the chicken herb filling:

2 tablespoons unsalted butter

2 tablespoons flour

1 cup low-sodium chicken broth

Salt, to taste

1 egg yolk

½ cup heavy cream

1 teaspoon Dijon mustard

8 ounces cooked, chopped chicken breast

¼ teaspoon fresh or pinch of dried tarragon

1 teaspoon fresh or dried chives

Freshly milled black pepper

4 (8-inch) crepes

½ cup grated Vermont white cheddar cheese

Make the crepes: Whisk together the flour and egg in a large mixing bowl. Gradually add the milk and water, stirring to combine. Add a pinch of salt and butter; beat until smooth. Let rest 30 to 60 minutes.

Heat a lightly oiled griddle or 9- to 10-inch frying pan over medium-high heat. Pour or scoop the batter onto the griddle, using approximately ¼ cup (2 ounces) for each crepe. Tilt the pan with a circular motion so that the batter coats the surface evenly. Cook the crepe for about 2 minutes, until the bottom is light brown. Loosen with a spatula, turn and cook the other side for about 1 minute.

Make the Mornay sauce: In a medium saucepan melt the butter over medium-high heat. Whisk in the flour and cook, whisking constantly, for about 1 minute. Do not allow it to brown. Slowly whisk in the milk and continue to whisk until the sauce thickens and comes to a boil, about 2 to 3 minutes. Reduce the heat to a simmer and season with the salt, pepper, and nutmeg. Allow to simmer for 2 to 3 minutes. Stir in the cheeses and whisk until melted and smooth. If the sauce seems too thick, thin with a little milk. Keep warm and ladle 2 ounces over each savory filled crepe.

Make the filling: Melt the butter in a saucepan, blend in the flour, then whisk in the broth and salt, and cook, stirring constantly, until thickened. Remove from the heat. Mix together the egg yolk, cream, and mustard. Stir a small amount of the cream sauce into the broth mixture, then stir back into the cream sauce. Cook over low heat a minute more, then stir in chicken and herbs, and season to taste with salt and pepper. Let it heat through and keep it warm.

Assemble the crepes: Position a rack about 6 inches below the broiler and then preheat it for 10 minutes. Fill each crepe with the chicken mixture and sprinkle grated cheddar cheese over the filling. Fold or roll the crepes over the filling and place them on a broiler-safe baking dish or platter. Broil 2 to 3 minutes. Ladle 2 ounces of Mornay sauce over each crepe and serve immediately

SOUTHERN RED VELVET CAKE

(MAKES 1 [10-INCH] 2-LAYER CAKE)

In keeping with its location and Deep South name, the baking at Magnolia includes a lot of traditional Southern fare, such as a pecan pie that has been featured twice by *Southern Living,* in its magazine and its food-lover's travel guide, *Off the Eaten Path.* Another popular sweet that has become almost a signature dish is this old-fashioned Southern staple.

For the cake:

Vegetable oil spray, for the pans
2½ cups all-purpose flour
1½ cups sugar
1 teaspoon baking soda
1 teaspoon fine sea salt
1 teaspoon cocoa powder
1½ cups vegetable oil
1 cup buttermilk, at room temperature
2 large eggs, at room temperature
1½ tablespoons red food coloring
1 teaspoon distilled white vinegar
1 teaspoon vanilla extract

For the cream cheese frosting:

1 pound cream cheese, softened
4 cups sifted confectioners' sugar
1 cup (2 sticks) unsalted butter, softened
1 teaspoon vanilla extract

Crushed pecans, for garnish

Make the cake: Preheat a convection oven to 320°F or a conventional one to 350°F. Lightly spray and flour two 10-inch round cake pans. In a large bowl, sift together the flour, sugar, baking soda, salt, and cocoa powder. In another large bowl, whisk together the oil, buttermilk, eggs, food coloring, vinegar, and vanilla. Using a stand mixer, mix the dry ingredients into the wet ingredients until just combined and smooth.

Divide the batter evenly between the prepared pans and place the pans in the oven, spacing them evenly apart. Bake, rotating the pans halfway through, until the cake pulls away from the sides of the pans and a toothpick inserted in the center comes out clean, about 30 minutes. Remove the cakes from the oven and run a knife around the edges to loosen them from the sides of the pans. One at a time, invert the cakes onto a plate and then reinvert them onto a cooling rack, rounded side up. Let cool completely.

Make the frosting: In a standing mixer fitted with the paddle attachment, or with a hand-held electric mixer and a large bowl, mix the cream cheese, sugar, and butter on low speed until incorporated. Increase the speed to high, and mix until light and fluffy, about 5 minutes. Occasionally turn the mixer off and scrape the down the sides of the bowl with a rubber spatula. Reduce the speed of the mixer to low. Add the vanilla, raise the speed to high, and mix briefly until fluffy, again occasionally stopping and scraping down the bowl.

Place 1 layer, rounded side down, in the middle of a cake stand (a rotating stand, if you have one, will make the job a lot easier). Using a palette knife or offset spatula, spread a layer of cream cheese frosting ¼- to ½-inch thick over the top of the cake. Sprinkle with pecans. Carefully set the second layer on top, rounded side down, and repeat with more frosting, and then spread the remaining frosting on the sides of the cake. Sprinkle the top with more pecans.

Though Spanish and French explorers both made early attempts to establish colonies in and around Beaufort in the mid- to late sixteenth century, these early settlements were doomed to fail almost before they began, and it was not until the English settled in Charles Town at the mouth of the Ashley River that Europeans gained a permanent foothold in the Carolinas. By the beginning of the eighteenth century, that foothold had extended south to Port Royal, and in 1711 the port town of Beaufort was founded. While it was never to become as large or as urbane as its older sister, Charleston, to the north, or its brash younger sister, Savannah, to the south, it was already well established when Savannah's river bluff was settled by Oglethorpe some twenty years later, and it rapidly became a choice coastal outpost for the area's wealthy rice planters who were looking to escape mosquitoes and the tedium of rural isolation in exchange for the cooling sea breezes and lively social scene of this growing port town of Beaufort. By the early nineteenth century, Charleston and Savannah were both larger than Beaufort, but this little town rivaled them in per capita wealth, and its streets were lined with graceful mansions.

Today, while urban redevelopment and the explosive growth of gated retirement communities have changed much of the face of the outlying countryside, the core of the old town remains remarkably intact and is a treasure trove of choice antebellum architecture. Travelers making their way along US Highway 17 as it winds through the scenic marshes from Charleston to Savannah frequently take a midpoint rest stop in this lovely historic town, visiting the waterfront and exploring such historic sites as St. Helena's Episcopal Church (1724), the serene, gracious veranda of the Greek Revival

Maxcy-Rhett House (1810), and, a few miles from town, the haunting ruins of Old Sheldon Church (see the photograph on page 106)—a spot that has the unique distinction of having been torched twice, by two different invading armies.

Now, everyone who has spent more than five minutes in this part of the world knows that Southerners don't consider a rest stop to be a real rest without a cold glass of sweet iced tea and a good lunch. Fortunately, there are two perfect places where visitors and locals alike go to get a taste of Beaufort's brand of Southern charm on a plate: Magnolia Bakery Cafe (page 107) overlooking the waterfront, and Shoofly Kitchen (page 147) on Boundary Street. Gracious hosts, charming atmosphere, and Southern cooking with a continental flare make each of these two breakfast and lunch cafes a standout—and well worth the stop.

Mrs. Wilkes' Dining Room

107 West Jones Street
(912) 232-5997
WWW.MRSWILKES.COM
Owner: Ryon Thompson

Jones Street, with its continuous canopy of overhanging live oaks, picturesque brick pavements, and historic architecture, has always been one of the most desirable addresses in Savannah. Of all its coveted residences, however, none is more desirable (at least as a destination) than 105–107 West Jones, a handsome pair of nineteenth-century row houses known collectively as The Wilkes House. Formerly a boardinghouse, its fame rests not in its location nor its graceful facade, but on the dining rooms and kitchen that fill its garden level. It's actually the easiest spot on the street to find: Once, when a visitor asked a local how to get to Mrs. Wilkes', they were told "just walk down West Jones until you smell fried chicken."

They might as easily have said, "Go down Jones until you see a long line of hungry-looking people—and get in it." That line, made up of as many locals as visitors, forms well before the door opens at eleven sharp, drawn in part by that aroma of chicken frying, and in part by a seamless reputation for first-rate Southern cooking of the sort that's rarely found anymore.

Since well before 1943, when she bought the building from her employer, until her death sixty years later, Sema Wilkes built her reputation feeding Savannah from that kitchen with old-fashioned, honest, and delicious Southern cooking. Still in the family, the dining room is now operated by her great-grandson Ryon Thompson, who diligently guards her legacy by making sure that the food and warm family atmosphere continue to meet her exacting standards. He even greets the first seating with the same blessing that his great-grandmother recited every day.

The guests, seated family style around large white-clothed tables, are an assortment of locals in business clothes and visitors in shorts, glamorous movie stars and uniformed utility workers—everything from presidents to kindergarteners. Shy, inhibited guests don't stay that way long. As heaped platters and bowls are passed and sweet tea is poured, the spirit of sharing is infectious. More than once, strangers from the same town—who live right down the street from one another—have met at these tables for the first time and left as fast friends.

The former boardinghouse on the upper levels is today divided into apartments, and tenants tend to stay put for years despite the bustle from the dining room below. One tenant whose apartment was just over the kitchen used to say he didn't need an alarm clock: The early-morning clang of pots, lively conversation, and sudden bursts of gospel singing from the cooks inevitably woke him on time. "My clothes always smelled like collard greens and fried chicken" he recalled, "and I didn't care!"

Mrs. Wilkes's fried chicken was already legendary, but it took on iconic proportions when she made it for Bryant Gumbel one morning on *The Today Show* and quipped, "If the Colonel had made it so good, he'd be a general."

It's so true—and thankfully, the chicken is still fried the same way.

Mrs. Wilkes' Famous Fried Chicken

(SERVES 4–6)

Most frying chickens nowadays are larger than they were in Mrs. Wilkes's heyday. Get the smallest bird you can, preferably less than three pounds.

1 (2½-pound) frying chicken, cut up
Salt and freshly milled black pepper
2 tablespoons evaporated milk
2 tablespoons water
Vegetable oil, for frying
All-purpose flour

Sprinkle the chicken with salt and pepper. Pour the milk and water over and let it marinate for about 10 minutes. Meanwhile, heat enough oil to cover the chicken (but no more than halfway up the sides of the vessel) to 300°F in a deep fryer or deep skillet over medium heat. One at a time, dip the chicken pieces in the flour and shake off the excess. Slip them into the hot oil and deep-fry, turning once and making sure that the oil completely covers the chicken at all times, until cooked through and golden brown, about 20 to 25 minutes.

MRS. WILKES' SQUASH CASSEROLE

(SERVES 8)

Hardened squash haters have been converted by this simple casserole. In the dining room, it is mounded into serving bowls, but you may serve it directly from its baking dish.

4 pounds yellow squash, sliced

1 medium onion, diced

1 teaspoon freshly milled pepper

1 teaspoon salt, plus additional for cooking squash

2 cups cornflakes, crushed

¼ cup (½ stick) unsalted butter, melted

1 (10½-ounce) can cream of mushroom soup

1 cup grated American cheese

Preheat the oven to 350°F. Combine the squash and onion in a saucepan with a little salted water. Cook over medium heat until tender, about 20 minutes. Drain and mash. Add the pepper, 1 teaspoon salt, cornflakes, butter, and soup and mix well. Pour into a 3-quart baking dish and cover with cheese. Bake 20 minutes.

Barbecue Pork

(SERVES 10–12)

1 (4- to 5-pound) pork shoulder roast

1 teaspoon salt

1 teaspoon freshly milled pepper

1 teaspoon paprika

2 cups water

For the spicy barbecue sauce (makes about 6 cups):

1 pint vinegar

Juice of 3 lemons

½ cup sugar

1 quart tomato ketchup

2 tablespoons salt

½ tablespoon ground cayenne pepper

¾ tablespoon black pepper

3 tablespoons prepared mustard

Tabasco Sauce, to taste (optional)

Preheat the oven to 350°F. Season the pork with salt, pepper, and paprika. Put it into a roaster and add the water. Cover tightly with foil and bake 1½ hours, or until fork tender. Remove from the pan and let cool enough to handle. Discard the liquid and fat remaining in the pan.

Remove the skin and excess fat from the pork. Using a pair of forks, "pull" or shred the meat into small pieces.

Make the barbecue sauce: Combine the vinegar, lemon juice, and sugar in an enamel-lined or stainless steel pot and bring it to a boil. Add the ketchup, salt, cayenne, pepper, mustard, and Tabasco to taste (if desired). Boil 5 minutes.

Mix the meat with a generous portion of barbecue sauce and return it to the roaster. Bake until heated through, about 30 minutes.

Savannah Coffee Roasters (wholesale only)

2700 Gregory Street
(800) 352-2994
www.savannahcoffee.com
Roastmaster: Hayden Banks

Founded in 1909 as the Savannah Coffee Company, Savannah Coffee Roasters is one of the oldest coffee importers/roasters in the region, and for decades it operated the only specialty coffee/espresso bars in the Savannah area. They became famous in the community and beyond for such unique flavored coffees as Southern pecan roast. Today, with a Starbucks on every other corner and a number of locally owned coffee bars in the mix, Savannah Coffee Roasters has returned to its roots and is strictly a wholesale dealer, providing uniquely blended and freshly roasted coffees to local supermarkets, gourmet stores, downtown gift shops, and even a few of those specialty coffee bars that used to be their competition. It is also the roaster and wholesaler for a line of specialty blended and flavored coffees by Paula Deen's husband Captain Michael Groover.

Perc Coffee

2424 De Soto Avenue (Starland Dairy District near Back in the Day Bakery)
(912) 209-0025
www.perccoffee.com
Owner/Roastmaster: Philip Brown

It is safe to say that Perc Coffee owner Philip Brown has changed the face of Savannah's restaurant industry. Before he opened his business, which specializes in organically grown coffees from environmentally conscious growers around the globe, most local restaurant coffee was almost an afterthought. Even some of the finest dining spots did little better than standard food-service coffee, indifferently brewed in automatic equipment. Today, thanks to Perc, everything from coffee bars to take-out cafes to the finest white-cloth dining rooms offer not just great coffee, but coffee that is uniquely blended for the personality of their business. Though the roasting facility is strictly a wholesale operation (Perc sells directly to the consumer only online and at the Forsyth Farmers' Market, page 101), visitors are welcome to tour the plant, learn about the coffee world, and sample a cup—or two. Perc coffee is also sold through a local specialty food stores such as FORM (page 77) and Kitchenware Outfitters of Savannah (see Kitchen Academics, page 50).

Ogeechee River Coffee Roasters

4517 Habersham Street (Habersham Village)
(912) 354-7420
www.ogeecheecoffee.com
Owner/Roastmaster: Scott Miller

A relative newcomer to Savannah's bourgeoning coffee-roasting industry, Scott Miller, who grew up in Savannah, became interested in coffee roasting while working in food service at a yacht marina in southern Florida. There he had to learn how to roast whole coffee beans for one of the yacht owners. He was soon hooked and discovered that there was a whole world of "coffee geeks" just like him. At first, it was only a hobby, but as he got deeper and deeper into perfecting his technique, and began to learn more about the difficult life of the world's coffee farmers, he decided to turn this expensive hobby into a business that would support small growers from around the globe. He opened Ogeechee River Coffee in nearby Statesboro, home to Georgia Southern University, but after he began to realize that most of his wholesale business was in his hometown, he decided to move back to Savannah. Now located in Habersham Village (page 20), the shop also contains a coffee bar (featuring breakfast fare and sandwiches from Thrive cafe, page 172), and has a small retail section, but the lion's share of his business remains wholesale to the food industry.

Noble Fare

321 Jefferson Street
(912) 443-3210
www.noblefare.com
Owners: Chef Patrick and Jenny McNamara

On the intersection of West Harris and Jefferson Streets, in the quiet west end of the Historic District, stands a trim little brick Victorian storefront that has had as many lives in Savannah's restaurant scene as the proverbial nine-lived cat. Today this handsome period building with wide, multipaned shop windows and wide, wrought-iron balcony is home to Patrick and Jenny McNamara's Noble Fare, a white-cloth restaurant styled on the classic family-run bistros common throughout France.

It's the fulfillment of a dream whose seeds were planted back when the McNamaras first met while working at Blake's Seafood Grille in Chagrin Falls, Ohio. Fueled by a common passion for fine food and wine, their courtship quickly led to marriage, and that, in turn, led them to dream of opening a restaurant where they could share their passion for food and wine with others while still having a normal family life. They moved to Savannah and, in 2007, made their dream a reality with the opening of Noble Fare.

The most frequently asked question is how they chose the name. It's mainly a nod to the Gaelic origins of their names: Patrick means "noble" and Jenny means "fair"; once they put the two together, it seemed only natural to take advantage of the play on words between fair and fare. In the bigger picture, however, what it really reflects back on is that dream of a family restaurant. Even the French decor of the dining room, which Chef McNamara describes as "heirloom chez grandmère," plays into the family theme: The crystal chandeliers, gilded mirrors, black-lacquered furniture, and red silk draperies do lend the feel of dinner in a French grandmother's dining room—though perhaps more like one in Creole New Orleans than Paris.

Despite his elegant and often elaborate presentations, Chef McNamara believes in keeping the food simple and fresh, and, while realizing the area can't yet provide everything, he aims to eventually be 100 percent local. "We don't have a walk-in cooler or freezer because we use only grade A-plus products and don't buy more than we can use right away. And we don't have a pantry because the only things we buy in cans are tomato paste and pineapple and cranberry juice."

His cooking style, he says, is straightforward. "What I do is the classics—using the classic French techniques. And I don't put anything on the plate that you aren't going to eat."

Duck-Duck-Duck-No-Goose

CRISPY DUCK BREAST WITH DUCK AU JUS, DUCK CONFIT RISOTTO
& PAN-SEARED FOIE GRAS

(SERVES 4)

4 boned but not skinned duck breasts

¼ teaspoon each freshly ground cinnamon, star anise, cardamom, fenugreek, and cumin

About 6 cups roasted duck au jus (see Duck Leg Confit Noble Fare—recipe page 122)

8–10 tablespoons unsalted butter, divided

¼ cup minced yellow onion

1½ cups carnaroli or other medium-grain rice

½ cup freshly grated Parmigiano Reggiano

Salt and freshly milled black pepper

1 cup shredded Duck Leg Confit Noble Fare (recipe page 122)

4 (2-ounce) slices duck foie gras

Preheat the oven to 500°F. Score the duck breast skin in a crisscross pattern with a sharp knife or razor blade. Rub well with the spice blend and set them aside.

To make the risotto: Bring the duck au jus to a simmer and keep it barely simmering. Melt 5 tablespoons butter in a heavy-bottomed dutch oven or pot over medium-high heat. Add the onion and sauté until it is golden. Stir in the rice and sauté, stirring almost constantly, until it is hot and coated with butter. Add ½ cup au jus and stir until the pan is almost dry. Add another ladleful of au jus, and again stir until the pan is almost dry. Repeat with more au jus until the rice is al dente and creamy, reserving 1 cup au jus for the reduction (if more than 5 cups of liquid are needed before the rice is done, finish it with water). Turn off the heat, stir in the cheese and then fold in the shredded duck confit. Season to taste with salt and pepper.

To prepare the duck breasts: Heat an ovenproof sauté pan over medium-high heat, add a little butter and put in the duck, skin down. Sear until the skin is browned, about 4 minutes. Turn the breasts skin up and transfer the pan to the hot oven. Roast until it is done to your liking (Chef McNamara serves it medium rare).

To plate: Divide the risotto among four warm serving plates. Put the duck breasts over the risotto, crisp skin up. Return the sauté pan to the heat and film it with butter. Sear the foie gras until it is browned on both sides (about a minute per side) and put a slice of it on each duck breast. Deglaze the pan with 1 cup reserved duck au jus, stirring and scraping to loosen any cooking residue, and boil until it is reduced to 4 tablespoons. Off the heat, thicken the reduction by whisking in a tablespoon or so of butter, then spoon the reduction around the risotto and serve immediately.

Gooseberry Gastrique
Alternate Sauce For Duck-Duck-Duck-No-Goose

(MAKES ABOUT 2 CUPS)

In the summer, Chef McNamara lightens the previous recipe a little by finishing it with a fresh seasonal gooseberry gastrique in place of the au jus reduction.

2 pints gooseberries
1 cup sugar
½ cup water
1 small cinnamon stick
1 sprig mint
Freshly squeezed lemon juice, to taste

Special equipment: **fine wire mesh sieve or *chinois***

Remove the papery outer skin from the gooseberries, rinse well under cold running water, and drain. Stir together the sugar and water in a saucepan. Add the cinnamon stick and bring it to a simmer. Simmer 10 minutes. Add the gooseberries, mint sprig, and lemon juice to taste and simmer until the berries are tender. Remove the cinnamon and mint, puree the berries, and strain them through a fine wire mesh sieve or *chinois*. Taste and adjust the lemon juice.

Duck Leg Confit Noble Fare

(SERVES 6)

4 whole duck legs (including the thigh)
½ cup minced shallot
2–3 cloves garlic, crushed, peeled, and minced
1 bulb fennel, trimmed, cored, and chopped
3–4 sprigs rosemary
Rendered duck fat and/or canola oil
⅓ cup each chopped onion, carrot, and celery, for the mirepoix

Preheat the oven to 275°F. Wipe the duck legs dry and put them in a heavy-bottomed dutch oven with fairly tall sides. Add the shallot, garlic, fennel, rosemary, and enough rendered duck fat to completely cover the duck (Chef McNamara follows traditional French practice and reuses rendered duck fat from the previous confit); if you don't have enough duck fat, supplement it with canola oil. Bake 4 hours, making sure that the fat barely simmers. If it bubbles too much, reduce the heat to 250°F. Remove it from the oven and let it rest 2 hours. Remove the duck from the fat while it is still warm, skin it, and remove the meat, reserving the bones for duck au jus (see below). Put the pulled confit into a storage container and completely submerge it in its cooking fat. Refrigerate until needed.

Make roasted duck au jus: Put the duck bones and a little fat in a rimmed roasting pan. Add 1 cup mirepoix (equal parts chopped onion, carrot, and celery), toss, and roast at 450°F until everything is well browned, about 30 minutes. Transfer the bones and mirepoix to a stockpot and add 6 cups water. Simmer at least 2 hours, strain, chill, and degrease. Keeps up to 5 days covered and refrigerated, or up to 3 months if frozen.

THE OLDE PINK HOUSE

23 ABERCORN STREET (AT REYNOLDS SQUARE)
(912) 232-4286
OWNERS: DINING GROUP SOUTH

Appropriately housed in one of the city's oldest surviving buildings, The Olde Pink House is one of Savannah's oldest continuously operating dining rooms. A local favorite for more than a hundred years, its culinary history began around the turn of the century with an old-fashioned Southern tearoom tucked into one of the downstairs parlors. Through the years, the tearoom expanded until it had occupied the entire ground floor and was eventually transformed into a white-cloth restaurant, which it has been for the last four decades.

Built in the late eighteenth century as a residence for James Habersham and his family, this handsome Federal-style building acquired an imposing neoclassical porch (and probably its signature pink stucco) when it became The Planters Bank early in the nineteenth century. Later divided into offices and shops, the building fell into such disrepair that by the 1930s it was facing almost certain demolition. Fortunately, the tearoom's determined proprietor, Alida Harper Fowlkes, rescued the building and eventually became one of Savannah's earliest and most ardent preservationists.

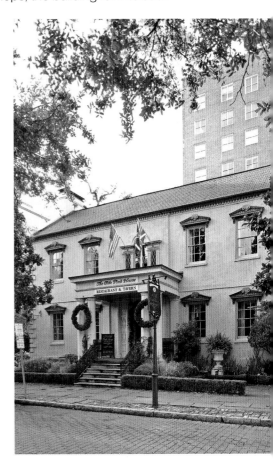

In the 1970s, the restaurant changed hands once more and, after extensive renovations, was reopened in its present fine-dining incarnation. In the early part of this century it was once again updated and refreshed, gaining a new wing that houses a modern kitchen, street-level bar, and opulent second-floor ballroom. Happily the original part of the house retains its stylish eighteenth-century decor and old Savannah atmosphere. Period antiques, crystal chandeliers, and handsome reproduction furniture fill the dining rooms, and the front entrance is still presided over by a vintage grandfather's clock and what is believed to be a portrait of its builder, James Habersham. For a real taste of Old Savannah, however, there is nothing else quite like a visit to the candlelit Planter's Tavern down in the cellar, with its brick walls, exposed ceiling rafters, and twin fireplaces, especially in the winter when those fireplaces are blazing.

Unlike many other restaurants of its kind, the menu here is not chef driven, but draws its identity mostly from its architecture and neighborhood, offering contemporary reinterpretations of traditional Southern fare.

Olde Pink House "BLT" Salad

(SERVES 4)

For the buttermilk thyme dressing (makes about 2¾ cups):

1 cup whole-milk buttermilk

1 cup mayonnaise

⅔ cup sour cream

1½ teaspoons dried thyme

1½ teaspoons freshly milled black pepper

2 teaspoons red wine vinegar

1 small clove garlic, finely chopped

½ teaspoon honey, or to taste

Salt, to taste

8 (¼-inch-thick) slices green tomato (about 2 large tomatoes with no hint of red or pink on them)

Salt

Buttermilk

1 cup all-purpose flour

1 cup stone-ground white cornmeal

Vegetable oil, for frying

8 slices thick-cut apple wood smoked bacon

Light brown sugar

4 cups mixed baby field greens or spring mix

1 cup buttermilk thyme dressing

½ cup chopped red bell pepper (stem, membranes, and seeds removed)

½ cup thinly sliced green onions

To make the dressing: Blend all the ingredients together, taste, and adjust the honey and salt. Keeps, covered and refrigerated for up to a week.

To fry the tomatoes: Sprinkle the tomato slices with salt and let them stand in a colander for 15 to 30 minutes. Wipe dry with paper towels, put them into a bowl, and completely cover them with buttermilk. Let stand another 15 to 30 minutes. Meanwhile, mix the flour and cornmeal together in a shallow bowl. Put enough oil in a deep skillet to cover the bottom by at least ¼ inch.

To prepare the bacon: Preheat the oven to 375°F. Fit a wire cooling rack into a rimmed sheet pan. Lay the bacon on a sheet of parchment or waxed paper and sprinkle it well with brown sugar, patting it into both sides. Shake off the excess and lay the bacon on the prepared pan, folding each slice to form a V shape. Bake until it is browned and crisp, about 15 minutes.

When you are ready to finish the salad, heat the oil in the skillet over medium-high heat to 365°F. Lift the tomato slices one at a time from the buttermilk, allowing the excess to flow back into the bowl, roll them in the flour and meal, shake off the excess, and slip them into the fat. Fry, turning once, until golden brown on both sides, about 5 to 6 minutes. Drain on paper towels.

To serve: Put the greens in a salad bowl, lightly coat them with dressing and toss. Divide the dressed greens among individual salad plates. Top with a fried green tomato, then the bacon, then a second fried green tomato. Garnish the top tomato with red pepper and green onions, drizzle with more dressing, and serve immediately.

CRISPY CORN BREAD OYSTERS
(SERVES 4)

These crisp and surprisingly light oysters are a popular appetizer at The Olde Pink House, topped with their own Green Goddess dressing, but they are equally popular served atop the Caesar salad as a substitute for the traditional croutons.

1 cup yellow cornmeal

1 teaspoon Old Bay Seasoning

½ teaspoon salt

¼ teaspoon white pepper

1 egg, lightly beaten

1 tablespoon half-and-half

Vegetable oil, for frying

1 pint shucked oysters, drained well

2 cups micro salad greens or baby field greens

Combine the cornmeal, Old Bay, salt, and pepper. Whisk together the egg and half-and-half. Add enough oil to a deep, heavy-bottomed pan or deep fryer to come halfway up the sides and heat it to 365°F. Dip half of the oysters in the egg and toss in the cornmeal mixture to cover well. Fry until crisp, 30 to 60 seconds, depending on desired degree of firmness. Drain on paper towels while frying the rest.

To plate and serve: Divide the greens among four serving plates, top with the oysters, and serve with Green Goddess dressing, cocktail sauce, or another sauce of your choice. Or serve them as they do at the Olde Pink House atop your own Caesar salad.

A Tale of Three Corner Diners

A reliable breakfast is usually the one meal that travelers can count on finding with no trouble at all: Most hotels offer it; fast-food outlets saturate the market with their own quick versions of it; it's the chain drive-in diner's bread and butter. But one of the charms of visiting a town is discovering that cozy corner mom-and-pop cafe where locals meet for morning coffee and a sweet roll, or to share a fortifying breakfast of bacon and eggs, pancakes glistening

with maple syrup, or biscuits smothered in sausage gravy—the sort of things that few have the luxury of time or metabolism to regularly have at home. For decades in downtown Savannah, that cozy corner spot was Clary's Drug Store (see Clary's Cafe, page 62), whose soda fountain/lunch counter was perpetually crowded by downtown characters from early morning until well after noon. Today there are at least three other such neighborhood cafes that fit the bill.

B. Matthews Eatery

325 East Bay Street
(corner of East Bay and Habersham)
(912) 233-1319
www.bmatthewseatery.com
Owners: Brian and Jennifer Huskey

B. Matthews is downtown Savannah's quintessential neighborhood restaurant. Owned by Brian and Jennifer Huskey, the energetic young couple who also own Blowin' Smoke BBQ (page 28), Abe's on Lincoln Tavern, and Blue Turtle Bistro on the Southside, it's open for breakfast, lunch, and dinner, has a full bar, and offers everything from homey breakfast biscuits smothered in gravy to hearty burger lunches to elegant evening wine tastings and late-night supper fare. Its best moments, however, may well be at breakfast, when the windows that face east onto Habersham let in the bright Lowcountry morning sun, and its air is fragrant with frying bacon, brewing coffee, and the irresistibly Southern aroma of baking scratch-made biscuits. This is the place to get shrimp and grits as it was originally served—for breakfast; hearty house-made hash browns and pancakes; and those fluffy, irresistible hot-from-the-oven biscuits, smothered with gravy or simply slathered with butter and jam.

Goose Feathers
Express Café & Bakery

39 Barnard Street (at Ellis Square)
(912) 233-4683
www.goosefeatherscafe.com
Owner: Beth Meeks

When Express Café & Bakery opened in 1986, this "gourmet in a hurry" corner cafe quickly became a staple with downtowners for breakfast and lunch. Now renamed Goose Feathers (inspired by its original goose logo), this neat, urban cafe remains a popular spot for locals and visitors, particular at midday on Sunday, when the place is filled to capacity with a suited and high-heeled after-church crowd rubbing elbows with late-rising T-shirt-and-shorts-clad bohemians and tourists. The menu here features sandwiches, quiches, pastries, and other breakfast fare that can be either made ahead or assembled and served quickly. Patrons may get their food fast, but they tend to linger at the tables over an extra cup of coffee or glass of iced tea, catching up with neighbors and meeting and advising visitors on local sightseeing.

Henry's Restaurant

Breakfast and Lunch
28 Drayton Street
(corner of Congress and Drayton)
(912) 232-6628
Owners: Hayndry "Henry" Prasetio and Liem Jian "Debbie" Hwee

Just across from historic Christ Church, the mother church of Georgia, is Henry's Restaurant, a bright little family-owned diner tucked into the back corner of Planter's Inn. With cheerful green walls and south-facing storefront windows running its length, Henry's matches the mood of its hardworking owners, who

are sunny and smiling even on the dreariest of days. They're the sort of people who, when no one could pronounce their names, cheerfully adopted the nicknames that their customers gave them: Henry and Debbie. Late risers need never worry about getting breakfast here: It's served from early morning until they close midafternoon, and, while the menu features the usual American diner lunch fare—burgers, chicken fingers, salads, and (this being the coast) fried shrimp—their real specialty is omelets—thin, almost crepe-like, omelets Asian style—folded over generous portions of a wide selection of all-American fillings, from ham and cheese to a mélange of seafood and vegetables.

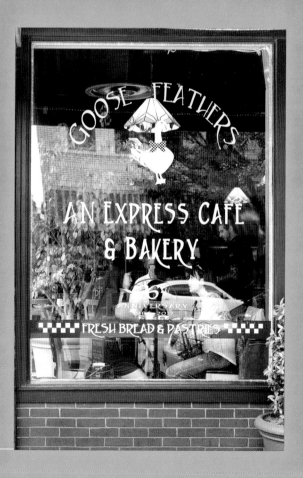

Papillote "French Cuisine to Go"

218 West Broughton Street
(912) 232 1881
www.papillote-savannah.com
Owners: Chef Hervé Didailler and Ann Marie Apgar

After working in some of the most prestigious restaurants in France and America, Chef Hervé Didailler had no interest in rising to the top of the celebrity-chef heap. Instead, he dreamed of a quiet little place where he could serve really good food without the

overhead, crazy hours, and high pressure of a "fine dining" establishment. It was not, however, until after he and partner Ann Marie Apgar visited and fell in love with Savannah that he began to take serious steps toward making that dream a reality. They pulled up roots, moved to town, and eventually opened this chic little take-out taste of France on Broughton Street.

Dominated by a large map of Paris hanging over the serving counter, French signage, and a bistro-style chalk menu board, Papillote may be in the heart of old Savannah, but its heart is as French as its chef/owner. Didailler grew up in Paris and, after studying at the École Supérieure de Cuisine Française, worked his way through the traditional restaurant apprentice system. In keeping with that training, but with the exception of a judicious selection of imported French wine, cheese, conserves, and confectionary, almost everything here is made in-house—from the brioche that accompanies the soup and forms the foundation for some of his signature sandwiches, to the authentic French macarons in the front case, to the marshmallows that top the house hot chocolate. There are also traditional pastries like the famous buttery Gâteau Breton and, on the weekends, fresh handmade croissants.

While the menu features such traditional Parisian bistro fare as Croque Monsieur (the sophisticated French version of grilled ham and cheese), Bouchée à la Reine (puff pastry filled with chicken, mushrooms, and spinach), and pommes frites simmered in duck fat, there are a number of original dishes. Little bits of Didailler's adopted home have crept into the mix as well. There's even an open-faced sandwich piled with brisket smoked by local Angel's BBQ (page 11). Nothing better illustrates this blending than his Duck Confit Pie, where a French pâte brisée tart shell is filled with the classic French Duck Conserve and Georgia-grown Vidalia Sweet Onions and Pecans.

Duck Confit Pie with Vidalia Onions & Pecans

(SERVES 8)

A key ingredient of this pie is rich, dark Banyuls vinegar, made with a sweet red wine from Banyuls-sur-Mer. Aged for at least five years in oak casks, its flavor is unique and has no real equivalent. Find it in select specialty groceries and food shops. Chef Didailler suggests serving this with a mixed green salad tossed with a simple vinaigrette.

For the pâte brisée (makes enough for 1 [10-inch] tart shell):

8 ounces pastry or all-purpose flour
½ teaspoon salt
½ cup (1 stick) unsalted butter, cut into bits
1 large egg yolk
About 3 tablespoons chilled water

For the spinach layer:

1 teaspoon butter
½ pound fresh spinach, washed and stemmed
1 clove garlic, minced
Salt and pepper, to taste

For the caramelized onion layer:

2 large Vidalia sweet onions
1 tablespoon olive oil
1 teaspoon unsalted butter
1 teaspoon sugar
Pinch of salt
Freshly milled black pepper, to taste
The leaves from 1 (3-inch) sprig fresh thyme

For the pear sautées:

3 Bosc pears, peeled, cored, and diced
1 teaspoon unsalted butter
2 tablespoons sugar
2 teaspoons Banyuls vinegar

8 duck legs confit, boned and pulled (available in specialty grocers and food shops)

For the spicy pecans:

2½ cups shelled Georgia pecan halves
About 2 tablespoons unsalted butter
2 teaspoons sugar
1 teaspoon powdered cumin
1 teaspoon salt
½ teaspoon ground cayenne pepper

For the caramelized pearl onions:

1 cup pearl onions, blanched and peeled
1 teaspoon unsalted butter
1 teaspoon sugar

Whole black pepper in a mill
Fresh flat-leaf parsley sprigs

Make the pâte brisée: Whisk together the flour and salt in a mixing bowl. Add the butter, cutting it into the flour until the mixture resembles coarse meal with bits of butter no larger than small peas. Mix in the egg yolk and water until it is just clumping together. Turn it onto a floured work surface and, with the heel of your hand, push it away from you, then gather and fold it, repeating until the liquid is evenly distributed. Do not overwork. Gather into a ball, cover with plastic wrap, and refrigerate for 1 hour before using.

Preheat the oven to 375°F. Roll out the pâte brisée to standard piecrust thickness and carefully lay it over a buttered tart pan or pie mold. Without stretching it, press it into the pan and trim off the excess. Cover with a sheet of parchment paper and weight with dried beans, raw rice, or ceramic pearl weights. Bake until it turns slightly golden on the edges, 20 to 25 minutes. Remove it from oven, remove the weights and parchment, and allow the pastry shell to cool completely.

When ready to continue, raise the oven temperature to 400°F.

Prepare the spinach: Heat the butter in a skillet or sauté pan over medium-high heat until lightly browned. Add the spinach and garlic and sauté until the spinach is wilted. Season with salt and pepper, remove from the pan, and drain well, gently squeezing to remove as much moisture as possible. Place the spinach in the pie shell and spread evenly over the entire bottom with a spoon.

Make the caramelized onion: Add the chopped Vidalia onions and olive oil to the skillet, and stir over medium heat until the majority of moisture is evaporated, then add the butter and sugar and continue sautéing until the onions are lightly caramelized. Season them with salt and pepper and mix in the thyme. Remove it from the heat and spread evenly over the pie.

Prepare the pears: Peel, core, and dice the pears, and add them to the skillet with the butter and sugar. Sauté until lightly caramelized. Deglaze the pan with the vinegar, remove it from the heat, and spread the pears evenly on top of the spinach and onions.

Lay the duck leg confit in a baking pan and put it in the oven for 1 minute to warm. Remove and quickly remove the excess skin, fat, bone, and cartilage. Break the meat apart and spread all over pie evenly and press lightly to compact the pie ingredients.

Prepare the pecans: Toast the pecans in the oven for 1 or 2 minutes, then transfer to the skillet with enough butter to lightly coat them, the sugar, cumin, salt, and cayenne pepper. Sauté until the nuts are entirely coated. Sprinkle over the pie.

Finally, prepare the caramelized pearl onions: Sauté the blanched onions with the butter and sugar over medium high heat until lightly caramelized, about 5 minutes or less, and spread them evenly over the pie.

To serve: Preheat the oven to 400°F. Cover the pie with aluminum foil and reheat in the oven for approximately 5 minutes. Remove it from the oven, uncover, and sprinkle it with freshly ground black pepper and a few sprigs of parsley..

Rancho Alegre Cuban Restaurant

402 Martin Luther King Jr. Boulevard
(912) 292-1656
WWW.RANCHOALEGRECUBAN.COM
Owners: Juan Manuel Rodriguez and Melody Rodriguez Schanely

The historic face of Savannah has been so dominated by Anglo-European culture and architecture that few people realize it has always been an ethnically diverse city. Yet, it's only in the last twenty years that that diversity has really begun to make a place for itself in the restaurant culture. One notable example of this trend is Rancho Alegre, a Cuban/Latin-American bistro on the west side of downtown.

Originally located in a tiny 1950s cottage on the Southside, in 2010 its current owners moved to its present location. Appropriately, it's in the heart of the newly revitalized West Broad Street (now MLK Jr. Boulevard) business district that, before desegregation, was once a strictly ethnic community.

With its sunny yellow walls trimmed in hand-painted Mexican tiles and punctuated by vintage Cuban advertisements and travel posters, its ceiling strung with festive lanterns and streamers, and the long banquette on the south wall scattered with pillows covered in South American fabrics, Rancho Alegre could be almost anywhere in the Caribbean basin. And that's exactly how its owners want it.

"Cuban, Venezuelan, Mexican Gulf—it's all similar," says Juan Manuel Rodriguez, a Venezuelan-born banker turned chef who tends the day-to-day operation of the restaurant (his daughter and partner is an administrator at Armstrong Atlantic University). While the main part of the menu is Cuban, Rodriquez likes mixing it up with dishes not only from his own country but gleaned from his travels throughout South America and Spain.

Cooking comes naturally for this jovial, gregarious man, who grew up in Tovara, Venezuela, just behind a bakery, and still daydreams of its *roskas,* colorfully decorated twice-baked biscotti-like cookie rings. While the day-to-day cooking is left to the staff, most weekends find him in the kitchen, roasting Spanish-

style suckling pig, making huge pans of seafood-studded paella, or frying up chunks of *chipen*—Spanish brined pork that has been simply seasoned with a rub of garlic, thyme, and salt and slow-baked until it is meltingly tender. It is then cut into chunks and deep-fried to crisp the outer skin.

"I eat fish and salad every day of the week," Juan sighs and then adds with a grin and a wink, "I make my sins on the weekend."

Savannah's resemblance to the Caribbean basin naturally invites Rodriguez to take advantage of the abundant fresh seafood in our area, preparing it in classic Caribbean–Gulf Coast style. Almost every culture throughout the region and up the Atlantic coast has some version of shrimp with garlic and wine, and Rancho Alegre's simple but delectable Caribbean version has a lot in common with an old Savannah dish of shrimp in a buttery sauce of garlic-scented sherry.

Camarones al Ajillo

Shrimp in Garlic & Wine Sauce

(SERVES 4)

6 tablespoons (¾ stick) unsalted butter

2 tablespoons coarsely chopped garlic

3 tablespoons chopped fresh parsley

2 pounds large shrimp, peeled (and deveined if desired)

Sazon Completa (see note)

1 cup dry white wine

Sweet paprika, to taste

4 leaves romaine or other leaf lettuce

4 cups hot cooked white rice

Melt the butter over medium-low heat. Add the garlic and 2 tablespoons parsley and simmer gently until the garlic is softened, about 3 to 4 minutes. Add the shrimp and toss until almost done (turning pink but still not quite opaque).

Season generously with Sazon Completa to taste, stir, and slowly add the wine. Raise the heat, bring it to a simmer, and cook until the shrimp are done and the wine has lost its sharp, alcoholic aroma. Turn off the heat, sprinkle with paprika to taste, and stir it into the sauce. Line four individual dishes with lettuce leaves and spoon the shrimp over them. Sprinkle with the remaining parsley and serve at once with white rice on the side.

Note: Sazon Completa, which means "Complete Seasoning," is a popular Latin American seasoning blend, available at Latino markets and many supermarkets.

Especial Rancho Alegre

(SERVES 4)

A slightly more complex dish, but no more difficult to make, is this specialty of the house, a mélange of local clams, shrimp, mussels, and grouper simmered in a spicy Creole sauce.

2 tablespoons olive or vegetable oil

½ green bell pepper, cored and coarsely chopped

½ yellow onion, peeled and coarsely chopped

1 tablespoon coarsely chopped garlic

2 cups fish stock

¼ cup tomato puree

2 tablespoons Sazon Completa (see note on page 135)

2 bay leaves

Salt and freshly milled black pepper

2 (10-ounce) grouper fillets, each cut in half

20 black mussels

8 large or 16 littleneck clams

20 medium shrimp, peeled and deveined

1 cup calamari cut into ½-inch-thick rings
   (about 2 large calamari)

4–8 leaves romaine or other leaf lettuce

2 tablespoons chopped parsley

4 cups hot cooked white rice

Put the oil, pepper, and onion in a large, heavy-bottomed pan over medium heat and simmer until the onion is softened, about 5 minutes. Add the garlic and simmer 1 minute, then add the stock, tomato puree, Sazon Completa, and bay leaves, and boil for 5 minutes. Taste and add salt and pepper as needed.

Add the grouper, mussels, and clams, bring to a simmer, and cook for 3 minutes. Add the shrimp and calamari and simmer until they are just cooked through, about 2 minutes longer. Divide the lettuce among individual gratin dishes, spoon the seafood and sauce over them, sprinkle with parsley, and serve at once with white rice passed separately.

ROCKS ON THE ROOF

THE BOHEMIAN HOTEL SAVANNAH RIVERFRONT
102 WEST BAY STREET
(912) 721-3800
WWW.BOHEMIANHOTELSAVANNAH.COM
OWNER: THE KESSLER GROUP
EXECUTIVE CHEF: ZACHARY MARTIN

One of the most popular destinations for Savannah's visitors is River Street, a cobblestone avenue at its name-sake river's edge, separated from the water by wide, brick-paved plazas and bordered by ancient warehouse buildings on the other. Once a bustling commercial area, by the mid-twentieth century the street had deteriorated into a rough

place that no sane local would go near—unless they were purposefully looking for trouble. As Savannah's downtown preservation movement gathered steam, however, it was clear that its riverfront needed attention before this critical element of the historic fabric was lost. The city therefore cleaned up the river, replacing the docks with a series of plazas and parks, and started the slow process of attracting developers to rescue the old warehouse buildings from oblivion. Though their brick and stuccoed facades retain their picturesque, weather-beaten character, today they're home to dozens of shops, offices, museums, nightclubs, fashionable restaurants, residential condominiums, and inns.

For decades after the riverfront's renaissance, however, a gaping hole remained just west of the Hyatt Hotel, leaving this end of the street looking a bit beleaguered and sad. All that changed with the construction of The Bohemian, a new luxury hotel that handsomely fills the gap with architecture paying homage to its ancient neighbors while remaining unapologetically modern. Crowning the roof of this fashionable hotel is Rocks on the Roof, the bar and casual, small-plate dining alternative to the hotel's main restaurant, Rocks on the River Modern Grill. With terraces that command panoramic views of the riverfront and breathtakingly magnificent sunsets beyond, live entertainment, and a tapas-style menu, this sleek, hip tavern has quickly become one of Savannah's most popular nightspots.

The small-plate offerings are a cosmopolitan mix of upscale bar food such as truffled fries and bruschetta made from focaccia-style bread but touched with local color from the likes of such regional favorites as fried green tomatoes, shrimp, and crab cakes. One popular offering is chicken and waffle sliders—a small-bite riff on a very old Savannah favorite.

Chicken & Waffle Sliders with Boursin Cheese & Strawberry Peppercorn Sauce

(SERVES 4–6)

For the waffles:

1¾ cups all-purpose flour
2 tablespoons sugar
1 tablespoon baking powder
2 large eggs
1¾ cups milk
½ cup vegetable oil or melted butter
1 teaspoon vanilla
Oil for brushing the waffle iron

For the chicken tenders:

1 cup all-purpose flour
2 cups Italian-style seasoned bread crumbs
Salt
Freshly milled black pepper, to taste
Ground cayenne pepper, to taste
1 large egg, beaten
½ tablespoon water
4 chicken tenderloins
2 quarts oil, for frying

For the Strawberry Peppercorn Sauce:

3 pints strawberries, washed and stemmed
1½ cups sugar
½ cup pancake syrup
2 tablespoons pink peppercorns

About ½ cup Boursin cheese, softened
   at room temperature
About 1 cup arugula, for garnish
Powdered sugar, for garnishing

Make the waffles: Combine the flour, sugar, and baking powder in a large bowl mixing bowl.

In a separate bowl, beat together the eggs, milk, oil, and vanilla. Make a well in the center of the dry ingredients and pour in the wet ingredients, stirring just until moistened. Brush a preheated waffle iron with oil and cook in batches until the waffles are browned and cooked through.

Make the chicken tenders: Place the flour in a shallow bowl. Beat the eggs and water together in another small bowl. Place bread crumbs in a separate shallow bowl and season with salt, black pepper, and cayenne. One piece at a time, coat the chicken in the flour, then the eggs, and then the bread crumbs, and set aside.

Heat the oil in a deep fryer to 375°F. In small batches, fry the chicken 6 to 8 minutes, or until golden brown and just cooked through. Remove and drain on paper towels.

Make the sauce: Combine all the ingredients in a saucepot and, bring to a boil. Reduce the heat and simmer 10 minutes.

Assemble the sliders: Place a small square or circle of the waffle on a plate. Spread the waffle with Boursin cheese. Top with a piece of chicken, then drizzle some of the sauce over the chicken. Take another piece of the waffle and spread with more cheese. Place the waffle on top of the chicken, cheese side down. At Rocks, the sliders are garnished with more sauce, and topped with a little arugula and a light sprinkling of powdered sugar.

Sammy Green's

1710 Abercorn Street (between 33rd and 34th)
(912) 232-1951
WWW.SAMMYGREENS.COM
Owner: April Sanderson

The restored row of late Victorian storefronts in the neighborhood of St. Paul's Episcopal Church, a serene, brick gothic enclave at the heart of the early twentieth-century neighborhood loosely known as Savannah's Edwardian District, has seen many incarnations during the last century. Some of the businesses have come and gone in a hurry, but one that has endured is Sammy Green's, a neat little storefront cafe whose trim white facade, basket-weave cafe tables, and bold yellow awning make it easy to find. Inside, a beaded-board wainscot, Victorian trim, and a polished wood floor look back to the building's heritage, but colorful artwork and a collection of cafe tables and chairs in a variety of styles lend a bohemian atmosphere that speaks to its popularity with the art students who drop in from several SCAD classroom buildings in the neighborhood (see Savannah College of Art and Design, page 146). In fact, the first thing that impresses about Sammy Green's incredibly clean and neat interior is the warm, neighborhood-cafe atmosphere, which is almost entirely owed to its owner, April Sanderson, an attractive, energetic young woman with a ready smile and easy charm. She's always happy to stop and explain an item on the menu, or help customers with a decision. "We're here to please," she says, and she means it. They will even deliver your order within the neighborhood. She explains with a grin, "So many of our customers that live around here say, 'Oh, please, I'm right around the corner from you—I'll just come pick it up.' But I'm from New York; people expect delivery from the place right downstairs from their apartment. If you don't bring it to them, they don't order. So, we deliver!"

The name, as you might have guessed, has nothing to do with someone named Sam: It's a summary of the menu, which is primarily made up of "Sammies" (sandwiches) and "Greens" (salads). Fresh flavors and unusual combinations dominate; as an option to the usual fries, they offer slim *haricots verts* simply dressed with freshly squeezed lemon juice and a little olive oil. And in the spirit of "we're here to please," many of the sandwiches offer several options for the main ingredient. Sanderson also likes changing up the menu—adding, for example, a whole page of sliders for a season, each with different combinations of condiments and always with a choice of brisket, chicken, or fish. A perennial favorite is the Mediterranean Chop Salad, which takes the old tomato-cucumber-olive-and feta combination, adds diced slow-cooked brisket or chicken, and ramps it up with tahini vinaigrette and other Mediterranean flavors.

Mediterranean Chop Salad

(SERVES 2)

For the tahini dressing:

¼ cup tahini
¼ cup freshly squeezed lemon juice
¼ cup olive oil
2 tablespoons plain yogurt
1 teaspoon salt
½ teaspoon freshly milled black pepper

For the salad:

1 head romaine, chopped
8 ounces cooked beef brisket or grilled chicken, cut into bite-size dice
4 ounces feta cheese, cut into bite-size dice

½ cup grape tomatoes
½ cup cucumber, seeded and diced
¼ cup green bell pepper, seeded and diced
¼ cup pickled banana peppers, finely diced
¼ cup kalamata olives, sliced
¼ cup canned chickpeas, rinsed and drained
A handful pita chips, broken into bite-size pieces

Whisk together the tahini, lemon juice, olive oil, yogurt, salt, and pepper. Toss together the romaine, brisket or chicken, feta, tomatoes, cucumbers, peppers, olives, chickpeas, and pita chips in a large bowl. Pour the dressing over it and gently toss to mix. Serve at once.

Sapphire Grill

110 West Congress Street
(912) 443-9962
www.sapphiregrill.com
Chef/Owner: Christopher Nason

One the most forward-looking chefs in Savannah's downtown Historic District, and certainly one of the leaders of its current farm-to-table movement, is Chris Nason, chef/owner of Sapphire Grill. Chef Nason came here in the early 1990s from Charleston, where he had been an integral part of that city's restaurant earth-to-table revolution as the executive chef of Anson's. But while buying local has been his guiding philosophy ever since he opened Sapphire Grill, he disagrees that it is the only answer. "I don't believe local's the only way to go. Yes, I like to use our area's products where I can, but there are just some things that can't be gotten locally. I still get my mushrooms from a farmer in Washington State; she supplies things that I can't get around here and, besides, I've been doing business with her for twenty years; that isn't going to change. You see, she's out where there aren't any restaurants nearby to 'buy local'; if people like me didn't buy from her, she'd be out of business."

Besides, as he points out, Southern cooking was America's original "fusion" cookery, combining as it did the cuisines of Europe, Africa, and, to a certain extent, Native America, but this was especially true of Savannah. Because it was a major port lying in the heart of the subtropical band that surrounds the globe, there was the added element of a lot of other cross-cultural influences and ingredients from subtropical regions such as Southeast Asia. If old Savannah had subscribed completely to using only local produce, its cuisine would have been very different.

Chef Nason's cooking at Sapphire Grill is his own reinterpretation of that Southern cross-cultural fusion. Contrary to the widely held—and false—perception of the South's cookery as heavy, limited, and muddled, he argues, "Real Southern food is vibrant and architecturally firm—each flavor has its own integrity that remains intact. There's a reason Savannah was called the Hostess City. Charleston and Savannah were dining destinations in those days—international celebrities, nobility, and politicians came here from all over the world—just to eat."

BENNE-CRUSTED BLACK GROUPER
WITH SWEET SOY

(SERVES 4)

A prime example of Chef Nason's deft reinterpretations of Savannah's antebellum traditions is his Benne Crusted Grouper, which has been on Sapphire's menu since the place opened in 1998. "Benne" is an old West African name for sesame seeds, which were introduced to the region by African slaves and remain integral to Charleston and Savannah cookery. In this dish, a local fish is crusted with benne seeds, pan seared, and served with a sweet soy sauce that is reflective of the culinary influences of Savannah's trade with the Far East.

1 cup all-purpose organic flour

1 cup panko (Japanese bread crumbs)

¼ cup black sesame seeds

¼ cup white sesame seeds

Sea salt and freshly milled white pepper

Canola or olive oil

4 thick (6-ounce) grouper steaks

For the sweet soy (makes about 2½ cups):

1 tablespoon sesame oil

4 garlic cloves

¼ cup minced shallots

1 teaspoon red pepper flakes

2 cups grade-A soy sauce

3 generous tablespoons orange blossom honey

½ cup rice vinegar

Juice of 4 limes

Juice of 1 orange

2 bunches chopped cilantro

Special Equipment: *chinois* or fine wire mesh strainer

Combine the flour, panko, and sesame seeds in a wide, shallow bowl. Season to taste with salt and white pepper. Have a second shallow bowl half-filled with cool water nearby. Film a heavy-bottomed skillet with oil and place it over medium-high heat. Dip the grouper, one piece at a time, into the water to moisten it, let the excess drip off the fish, and roll it in the breading. Gently shake off the excess and, when the oil is almost smoking hot, slip the breaded grouper into the pan. Cook until the bottom is golden about 2 to 5 minutes, carefully turn it, and continue until the second side is golden and the fish is just cooked through.

Make the sweet soy: Add the sesame oil to a medium saucepan and bring to high heat. Add the garlic cloves and lightly brown. Add the shallots and red pepper flakes and lightly brown. Add the soy sauce, honey, vinegar, and lime and orange juices, and bring to a boil over medium-high heat. Immediately reduce the heat to a low simmer and let it simmer until it is reduced by one-third. Remove from the heat and let cool, then strain it through a *chinois* or fine wire mesh strainer and add chopped cilantro.

Transfer the fish to warm plates and dot the plate with sweet soy. Serve immediately.

SAVANNAH COLLEGE OF ART AND DESIGN

A major force in the preservation and restoration of Savannah's historic downtown is the Savannah College of Art and Design, or simply "SCAD," as it is known locally. Founded in the spring of 1978, this private art college is still actively presided over by one of its cofounders, Paula S. Wallace. The college's commitment to, and active role in, the downtown preservation movement began almost immediately, when in 1979 it acquired a major downtown monument as its first building—the 1892 Romanesque Revival Savannah Volunteer Guard Armory on Madison Square.

Since those modest beginnings, the college has grown to become one of the largest private art schools in America, with three satellite campuses in Atlanta, Lacoste (France), and Hong Kong, offering comprehensive programs in every art form imaginable from the traditional disciplines of painting, sculpture, and architecture to dance, filmmaking, and fashion design. Its colorful, imaginative students have brought new sparkle to downtown life, but the real benefit for the historic downtown has been the college's commitment to preservation. It has rescued and renovated dozens of endangered historic buildings across the district and beyond, from a pre–Civil War railroad station, to late Victorian public school buildings and an Art Deco movie theater.

A subtle but no less critical contribution of the college to downtown life has been in the restaurant community, where its global student population has generated a truly international smorgasbord. From ethnic diners such as Al Salaam Deli (page 4) that have blossomed to satisfy homesick students with a taste of home, to those established by students who came here to study art and found a different love in cooking (see Cafe 37, page 38), to funky cafes opened by enterprising undergrads who just needed money for art supplies, the college's diverse student population has been a major factor in the changing face of Savannah's restaurant scene.

Shoofly Kitchen

1209 Boundary Street
Beaufort, SC
(843) 379-9061
www.shooflykitchen.com
Owners: Rose Anne and David Steele

There's no direct or easy way to get from Charleston to Savannah. The highway linking the two cities meanders lazily through the Lowcountry marshlands and sleepy little villages—and efforts by the state highway department to make it less of a meander keep long stretches under perpetual construction, slowing traffic even more. While the scenery is spectacular, it is not a route to take if you're in a hurry, so travelers making their way from one to the other take their time and frequently go a little out of the way to stop in Beaufort (see Historic Beaufort, page 112), a historic little port town that, while small, rivals its bigger sisters for fine old architecture and Southern charm. A lunch stop to unwind is, of course, essential, and there is no place better for that than Rose Anne and David Steele's charming breakfast and lunch spot, Shoofly Kitchen.

Though furnished like a typical shopping-center diner, with booth seating down one wall and a lunch counter surrounding its open kitchen, there is nothing typical about this place, and its atmosphere is relaxed and homey. In fact, if you feel as if you could slip off your shoes and put your feet up, why, that's exactly how Rose Anne and David want you to feel—as if you're at home.

Part of the reason for this atmosphere, no doubt, is because the Steeles haven't been restaurateurs their entire lives. But after long careers in high-end construction and real estate, they were weary of the economic uncertainties of those businesses and began looking for a change of pace. David had always loved cooking, and Rose Anne was an avid home baker, and since they were constantly entertaining at home— casual evenings with friends gathered like family in their kitchen—a cafe seemed like the perfect fit. Rose Anne had already done a lot of catering on the side, so they had no romantic illusions about the hard work involved. Their one romantic bent was that they did want their cafe to feel more like a home than a business. Rose Anne explains, "We have 'kitchen' in our name because we wanted our customers to feel like they were in a kitchen—our kitchen, rather than a cafe. Everything is open here, and customers love to sit at the bar and see what David is cooking on the stove."

As for the "Shoofly" part of the name, everyone assumes that it has to do with the famous pie, but it doesn't: It goes back to Rose Anne's grandmother, who used to sing the old song "Shoofly, Don't Bother Me" to Rose Anne's mother while churning butter on the porch. Rose Anne's mother in turn sang the song to her, and eventually she passed the legacy on to her own daughters by singing it to them. She says, "I always have to explain right away that I'm a Southern girl and always have been, and shoofly pie is a Pennsylvania Dutch pie."

As dyed-in-the-wool Southerners, the Steeles wanted Shoofly to be a truly Southern cafe, but without the stereotypical heavy food usually associated with such places. They also had a number of vegetarian and vegan friends for whom eating out in a small city like Beaufort was a challenge. The menu at Shoofly therefore emphasizes lighter, healthful, fresh ingredients, cooked in an unapologetically Southern style but with a lighter touch, with a number of dishes that everyone, from their vegan friends to the most hardened carnivore, can enjoy. There is no deep fryer in the kitchen, and the only "frying" David does is on his griddle—making the eggs and home fries served at breakfast and brunch.

Shoofly's Special Turkey & Cheddar Sandwich with Apple Chutney & Bacon

(SERVES 4)

Shoofly's apple chutney is a condiment you'll want to have on hand for things other than this turkey sandwich—roasted poultry of any kind, roast pork, pan-fried pork chops, grilled and sautéed sausages, and more.

For the Shoofly Kitchen apple chutney (makes about 10 cups):

2 pounds Gala apples, peeled and cored

1 large onion, chopped

⅔ cup (packed) light brown sugar

½ cup orange juice

3 tablespoons unsalted butter

2 teaspoons whole mustard seed

¼ teaspoon ground ginger

1/8 teaspoon ground cloves

2 cups dried cranberries

8 slices wheat berry bread

2 cups (16 ounces) Shoofly Kitchen apple chutney

16 ounces thinly sliced roasted turkey

4 ounces thinly sliced white cheddar

12 slices cooked bacon

Make the chutney: Combine all the ingredients in a large, heavy-bottomed saucepan, bring to a boil over medium heat, then reduce the heat to low and simmer 30 minutes. Let cool, then mash with a potato masher, leaving some chunks.

Cover one side of each slice of bread with 2 ounces (¼ cup) apple chutney. Place the turkey, cheese, and bacon on top of the chutney on half the slices of bread. Top with the remaining bread, chutney side down. Cut in half on the diagonal and serve.

Sweet Potato Hash with Spicy Hollandaise

(SERVES 4)

A popular brunch dish is the house sweet potato hash, spiked with bacon, topped with poached eggs, and drizzled with a spicy version of traditional hollandaise.

3 medium sweet potatoes, peeled and
    cut into ½-inch pieces

Salt

8 slices bacon

1 medium onion, peeled and chopped

Freshly milled black pepper

2–4 tablespoons maple syrup, to taste

¼ cup cider vinegar, plus more to taste as needed

For the spicy hollandaise:

½ pound (2 sticks) unsalted butter

3 large egg yolks

½ teaspoon ground cayenne pepper

½ teaspoon chili powder

1 tablespoon lemon juice

Salt and freshly milled black pepper

8 poached eggs

Cook the sweet potatoes in boiling salted water until just tender, about 3 minutes; drain. Cook the bacon in a heavy-bottomed skillet over medium heat. Remove the bacon, let cool, roughly chop, and set it aside. Spoon off most of the drippings, leaving about a tablespoon in the pan. Add the onion to the reserved drippings and sauté until it is lightly caramelized. Combine it with the sweet potatoes and season with salt and pepper, then add 2 tablespoons syrup and ¼ cup vinegar, taste, and adjust the seasonings, syrup, and vinegar accordingly. Refrigerate until chilled.

To make the hollandaise: Prepare the bottom of a double boiler with water and bring it to a simmer. Put the butter in the top of the double boiler and melt it over the simmering water. Whisk in the egg yolks, one at a time, until each is incorporated and the sauce is thickened. Add the cayenne, chili powder, and lemon juice, and season with salt and pepper to taste. If needed, a few drops of warm water can be added to adjust the consistency. Keep warm over hot water.

To serve: Sauté the sweet potato hash in bacon drippings until hot through and browned. Mix in the bacon and divide it among four warm serving plates. Nestle 2 poached eggs on each serving and top with spicy hollandaise.

Savannah's Candy Kitchen

225 East River Street
(912) 233-8411
318 West St. Julian Street (across from Belford's)
(912) 201-9501
www.savannahcandy.com
Owner: Stan Strickland

Stan Strickland has known the sweet life since he was a small boy in Woodbine, Georgia, sneaking homemade candy from his mother, who, despite working long hours in a local candy factory that specialized in pralines, pecan log rolls, divinity, and brittles, was an avid home candy maker

as well; she always seemed to be in her kitchen making pralines, brittles, divinity, and homemade baked goods, especially during the holidays. Fortunately, Stan did more than sneak treats: He also learned to make them. And when he grew up and came to live in Savannah, nothing seemed more natural than to share those treats with his neighbors by opening his own candy store. For the last thirty years, he has been feeding the sweet tooth of locals and visitors by the thousands in his landmark candy shop on River Street, the company's second downtown store on St. Julian Street in City Market, and, more recently from remote shops in Atlanta and Nashville.

With its vintage, brightly polished copper kettles, vast slabs of white Georgia marble, and a still-operating antique taffy-pulling machine out in the open, Savannah's Candy Kitchen's two downtown locations are almost like candy museums for visitors, who are welcomed and encouraged to stop and watch as they churn out scratch-made, creamy-rich Savannah pralines, crackling pecan and peanut brittles, glazed nuts, meltingly tender divinity, old-fashioned pulled taffy, and handmade chocolates by the ton. Most days Stan can still be found in the River Street shop, making candy, greeting customers, and simply reveling in the heady, mingled aromas of caramelizing sugar, warm chocolate, and toasting pecans, because, after all these years, candy making still holds a peculiar magic for him that he loves to share.

The Candy Kitchen's main focus is, of course, candy, especially its signature pralines; however, the sweet treats don't just stop there. The Kitchen also offers a selection of house-baked brownies, cakes, cookies, sweet breads, and, of course, that Southern staple, pecan pie.

Sol Fusion Restaurant

OWNER: ANDREA HADLEY
EXECUTIVE CHEF: MAREK ZARNOW

Sipping a margarita or glass of tequila while nibbling tacos and flatbread in the courtyard or airy, louvered dining area of Sol Fusion, a little islands-tropical cafe just north of 37th Street, you would never guess that this was once a dilapidated garage and gas station in the middle of a transitional, early twentieth-century neighborhood. Indeed, one almost expects to feel sand between the toes and hear waves crashing against the opposite edge of Habersham Street.

The atmosphere is that of a family-run taqueria, thanks to owner Andrea Hadley, a native Savannahian who seems to have been born with restaurant-business DNA running through her veins. Blending that keen instinct with a familial, almost maternal, affection for her employees, she's created a restaurant family that bonds by going bowling every Wednesday night after work.

But this is a taqueria like you will have never experienced. Taking inspiration from the spice trading routes of the fifteenth and sixteenth centuries that linked Latin America, Africa, and Europe with the Far East, blending spices, curries, and other exotic seasonings from every corner of the globe, Hadley and Executive Chef Marek Zarnow like mixing things up. They're often found working side by side in the kitchen, strategizing about new ways to celebrate that zesty fusion theme. As a result, you might get a tortilla topped with Korean barbecued pork and kimchee or flatbread with Thai shrimp in coconut red-chile sauce.

"We try to educate people," says Hadley, "and a six-inch flour tortilla is the perfect platform to get someone to try something new. You come in and you expect something else. I think about the food the same way I think about the wine we serve here. Every-

thing is served by the glass, so people don't lock in on one kind of wine."

It's a delicious and winning combination that consistently draws an eclectic crowd of seniors, families, neighborhood regulars, young professionals, and fortysomethings back to an outdoor dining courtyard and colorful art-studded dining room that on good days are opened up to flow together seamlessly.

In addition to its signature flatbreads and tacos, Sol Fusion serves an array of salads and regular sandwiches. At the bar you'll find more than sixty tequilas. That's a lot of tequila. Some of it goes into the cooking, in such things as this Tequila-Lime Skirt Steak Salad, a delectable balance of tart lime balanced with sweet orange, cooling crunch of jicama contrasting with warm steak, and lettuce and the smooth, aromatic bite of blue cheese. All components can be prepped in advance and compiled at the last minute, making it perfect for easy entertaining or a family meal.

As of this printing, Sol Fusion Restaurant has sadly closed its doors. Recreate this family-fun taqueria at home by making the Tequila-Lime Skirt Steak Salad provided here.

Tequila-Lime Skirt Steak Salad

(SERVES 4)

For the tequila-lime dressing (makes about 2¼ cups):

1 ounce tequila (preferably Jose Cuervo Gold)
1 ounce triple sec
½ teaspoon chopped fresh mint
1 ounce agave nectar
2 teaspoons whole grain mustard
Zest and juice of 2 limes
Juice of ½ navel orange
1½ cups mayonnaise
Salt and freshly milled black pepper

For the jicama slaw:

1 large jicama root, peeled and julienned
1 chipotle pepper packed in adobo sauce, minced
Orange juice

For the lime-marinated steak:

½ cup vegetable oil
1 clove of garlic
Zest of 1 lime
½ teaspoon freshly milled black pepper
4 (6-ounce) portions skirt steak

For the caramelized onions:

3 tablespoons butter
2 tablespoons olive oil
3 Vidalia or other sweet onions, julienned
Salt and freshly milled black pepper
2 teaspoons light brown sugar

2 romaine lettuce heads, washed and cut in half
About ½ cup crumbled blue cheese

Make the dressing: Using a blender on low speed, mix together the tequila, triple sec, mint, agave, mustard, citrus juices and zest, and mayonnaise until fully incorporated. Do not overblend or the mayonnaise could break. Season to taste with salt and pepper and pulse to blend. Cover and refrigerate until needed; it will keep for up to a week.

Make the jicama slaw: In a glass or nonreactive stainless steel bowl, combine the jicama, chipotle pepper, and enough orange juice to just cover the vegetable. Let marinate at least 4 hours.

Prepare the lime-marinated steak: Combine all the ingredients, add the steak, and marinate 1 to 3 hours.

Make the caramelized onions: Melt the butter in the olive oil in a large skillet over medium-high heat. Add the onions and salt and pepper to taste, and cook, stirring constantly, until the onions begin to soften, about 5 minutes. Stir in the sugar and cook until the onions are golden brown, about 20 minutes. Turn off the heat.

Prepare a grill with coals or preheat a gas grill. Grill the marinated skirt steak, turning once, to the desired temperature (about 125°F for medium rare). Remove from grill. Cover and let rest for 5 minutes while grilling the lettuce: Place romaine lettuce on grill, cut side down, and grill until warm and slightly beginning to wilt. Transfer to individual serving plates.

Slice the skirt steak on the bias and divide it on top of the grilled side of the lettuce. Top it with caramelized onions, jicama slaw, a sprinkling of blue cheese, and then drizzle with tequila-lime dressing.

FraLi Gourmet LLC

2700 Gregory Street, Suite 180
(912) 234-4644
www.fraligourmet.com
Owners: Chef Franco and Lisa Marra

For decades after Americans at large rediscovered authentic Italian cooking, and pasta became almost as commonplace here as it was in Italy, Savannahians who wanted quality, handmade fresh pasta still had to make it at home. That has finally changed since Chef Franco and Lisa Marra, makers of handmade pasta, authentic Italian conserves, and all-natural sauces, opened FraLi Gourmet. The Marras are no strangers to Italian food: Chef Franco is Italian, and the couple owned and operated a restaurant in that country for more than a decade. After moving to America, they dreamed of opening an emporium where they could offer the kind of high-quality food products they had known in Italy, so that busy mothers like Lisa, who was herself struggling to balance a hectic work schedule and still feed her family healthfully, could put dinner on the table without resorting to fast food. As she puts it, "I knew back then that busy moms needed food fast, not fast food."

The opportunity to make that dream happen came in an unexpected way, in the form of what seemed like a terrible setback: Chef Franco was laid off from his restaurant job. Despite the economic recession that had led to that layoff, the Marras decided that it was now or never, so they gathered their resources and established FraLi Gourmet. Then, just five weeks after they opened, another setback struck when Lisa was diagnosed with cancer. Determined to beat the disease, she mounted a vigorous fight supplementing conventional medical treatment with a rigorous diet of wholesome, natural food. Today she is cancer free, and the Marras have once again used what seemed like a terrible setback to their benefit: Lisa's successful battle galvanized their commitment not just to quality, but to making their products the most wholesome and healthful of their kind in the market. That commitment has paid off. Today, FraLi's exceptional pastas are used by the chefs of fine-dining restaurants all over town, including those who, like Italian chef Roberto Leoci (Leoci's Trattoria, page 92), also make fresh pasta in-house. FraLi's products can be found in a number of gourmet retail stores (such as FORM, page 77) as well.

FraLi's fresh pastas include a wide variety of ravioli with such fillings as spinach and ricotta, mushroom, lobster, pumpkin, and grilled vegetables, but they also offer a large selection of specialty dried pasta, from traditional spinach, porcini mushroom, and basil and tomato to unusual flavored pastas made with chocolate, peaches, and pomegranates. They also produce eggplant, mushrooms, mixed peppers, and giardiniera preserved in olive oil, as well as a variety of all-natural pasta sauces. From now on, "spaghetti night" for Savannahians will never be the same.

Starland Dining Group

WWW.STARLANDDINING.COM

OWNERS: CHEF MICHAEL PRITCHARD AND JOHN DEADERICK

STARLAND CAFE

11 East 41st Street
(912) 443-9355

CAFE ZEUM

The Jepson Center (Telfair Academy)
207 West York (corner of Barnard at Telfair Square)
(912) 790-8834

With its lush, subtropical, picket-fenced garden and shady, vine-covered front porch, Starland Cafe is the embodiment of the words urban oasis. Located at the edge of the commercial Starland Dairy District, this carefully restored and brightly painted late Victorian frame house sits in the middle of a short block of residences that miraculously survived the area's mid-twentieth-century commercialization. Passing through its garden gate onto that generous, shade-dappled porch, with its bright chalkboards and inviting garden furniture, is like passing through a tropical warp directly onto one of the fan-cooled verandas of old Key West. Inside, boldly painted accent walls, colorful original artwork, and neon-colored chalk menu boards continue the laid-back Margaritaville feeling, and that's exactly how its proprietors, Chef Michael Pritchard and John Deaderick, want it to be.

Oddly enough, these two fell into the cafe business almost by accident. Ardent preservationists, they live just across the street in a house that they had restored themselves. After they bought and restored this building, it was leased for several years to a coffee shop. When the coffee shop let its lease expire, however, they decided not to rent the space again, but to take the plunge and reopen the place themselves. Gradually, it grew organically from bohemian coffeehouse into a lunch cafe that not only thrived, but eventually generated a second sister cafe downtown.

In direct contrast, Cafe Zeum (ZEE-uhm), located in the soaring atrium of the Jepson Center, Telfair Academy's modern art wing, is as sleek, urban, and sophisticated as Starland is laid-back. When the museum approached Michael and John about taking over their cafe, it was an unexpected fulfillment of a long-term dream the two had shared to actually open a cafe in a museum, thereby combining their love of food, art, and architecture. Previously tucked away in a second-level space, the cafe was only marginally successful, but after Michael and John convinced the museum to move it into

the atrium, it has really taken off. Its contemporary furnishings, in keeping with the center's minimalist architecture by award-winning architect Moshe Safdie, were specially designed for the space, whose main decoration is an unobstructed view of Telfair Square and the historic Greek Revival facade of Trinity Methodist Church. And while both restaurants share an identical menu, the presentation at Zeum is appropriately uptown and sophisticated.

The specialty at both cafes is authentic panini on house-made ciabatta bread, with fillings ranging from traditional rosemary ham and chicken to Greek-style marinated asparagus. There is also a selection of fresh salads, including the signature Kitchen Sink, a mélange of marinated, roasted, and blanched vegetables, apples, grapes, and raisins enrobed in buttermilk dressing and topped with crisp noodles. Daily changing seasonal soups and hot plate specials, and platter combinations featuring house-made hummus, pimiento cheese, or a wedge of goat cheese round out the menu. The most popular item at both cafes, however, is their pesto chicken salad, which is served two ways—as a plated salad garnished with fire-roasted tomatoes, artichoke hearts, and red onion, and as a panini.

Drunken Cheddar & Corn Chowder

(SERVES ABOUT 8)

4 tablespoons (½ stick) unsalted butter

1 onion, minced (about 1 cup)

2 carrots, peeled and chopped fine (about 1 cup)

2 medium garlic cloves, minced

⅓ cup unbleached all-purpose flour

1¾ cups low-sodium chicken broth

1 12-ounce bottle beer

2 cups whole milk

12 ounces sharp cheddar cheese, shredded
    (about 3 cups)

4 ounces American cheese, shredded (see Note)

2 teaspoons cornstarch

1 teaspoon dried chipotle powder

Salt and pepper to taste

About 1 cup chopped cooked chicken or shrimp
    (optional)

About 2 cups fresh cooked corn, freshly cut from
    the cob, or canned

About ½ cup chopped cilantro

1 large loaf fresh artisan bread with a crust,
    cut into small pieces for dipping

Melt the butter in a large dutch oven over medium heat. Add the onion and carrots and cook until lightly browned, 8 to 10 minutes. Add the garlic and cook until fragrant, about 30 seconds. Stir in the flour and cook until golden, about 1 minute. Slowly whisk in the broth, beer, and milk. Bring to a simmer, then reduce the heat to low and simmer gently (do not let it boil) until the carrots are very soft, 20 to 25 minutes.

Meanwhile, toss the shredded cheeses, cornstarch, and chipotle seasoning in a large bowl until well combined. Puree the soup in a blender in batches until completely smooth, return to the pot, and simmer over medium-low heat. Whisk in the cheese mixture, a handful at a time, until smooth. Season with salt and pepper to taste.

A great addition to this soup is a cup or so of cooked, chopped chicken or shrimp. Stir it in at this point and let it just heat through. Garnish with corn and chopped cilantro and serve with bread. A spoon is optional. This dish keeps, covered and refrigerated, for up to 5 days. Gently reheat over medium-low heat, stirring often to prevent scorching, and don't let it actually boil.

Note: You will need a 4-ounce chunk of American cheese from the deli counter; do not use presliced or packaged shredded cheese. Freeze the American cheese for 20 minutes to make shredding easier.

Starland's Red Grape Chicken Salad

(SERVES 8)

4 pounds skinless, boneless chicken breasts,
   trimmed of excess fat

Olive or vegetable oil, for cooking the chicken

Salt and freshly milled black pepper

1 cup mayonnaise (Duke's preferred)

¼ cup fresh basil pesto, homemade or purchased

1 tablespoon Dijon mustard

1 tablespoon dried Italian herbs

1 tablespoon dried garlic-and-herb seasoning

¼ cup chopped fresh parsley

1½ cups crosswise-sliced seedless red grapes

Optional ingredients for serving as a main dish:

3 pounds fresh mixed salad green

3½ cups (28 ounces) balsamic salad dressing

8 ounces red grapes, sliced crosswise

16 marinated artichoke hearts

32–40 grape tomatoes, halved

1 red onion, chopped

Position a rack in the middle of the oven and preheat to 400°F. Line a rimmed sheet pan with foil and lay the chicken breasts on it in one layer. Brush them with oil and sprinkle generously with salt and pepper. Roast until a meat thermometer inserted into the thickest part of the breast registers 160°F, about 20 minutes. Remove it from the oven and allow it to cool until it just feels warm, but not hot.

While the chicken is cooking mix together the mayonnaise, pesto, mustard, dried herbs, garlic-and-herb seasoning mix, parsley, and grapes in a large bowl. When the chicken is ready, shred it into bite-size pieces using two forks, add it to the other ingredients, and mix thoroughly. Season as needed with salt and pepper. Serve at room temperature or lightly chilled, either as a sandwich spread or a plated main-dish salad as follows:

Toss the salad greens with the optional balsamic dressing and divide them among eight salad plates. Divide the chicken salad among the salad greens and scatter the grapes, artichoke hearts, and tomatoes around it. Top each with a large pinch of red onion.

THE SUNDAE CAFE

304 1st Street
Tybee Island
(912) 786-7694
WWW.SUNDAECAFE.COM
Owners: Kevin Carpenter and A. J. Baker

Like so many places throughout the South, this popular beach town bistro has a name that makes perfect sense to locals but bewilders anyone from outside its close-knit community. Fortunately, also like so many Southern places with odd names, there's a story behind this one. The short version is that the cafe was originally an ice cream parlor and sandwich shop. It was so popular with locals and visitors alike that, when the present owners bought it, they kept the name and, at least for a while, the ice cream bar. The kitchen and dining room, however, they gradually took in a completely different direction. As the emphasis shifted from sandwiches, ice cream cones, and milk shakes to sit-down lunches and dinners, the dining room got bigger and more formal while the ice cream bar got smaller and eventually went completely way.

Given its name and unassuming location (in a strip shopping center right next to a convenience store and row of gas pumps), few newcomers who cross its threshold are prepared for what they find inside: a casually elegant, white-cloth dining room where some of the best seafood and upscale comfort food in the area is served. Though the dining room is dressy, there's no dress code to speak of; you'll rarely see men in jackets (except when the weather is cool), and there are as many patrons in dresses and slacks as shorts and sandals.

Here the emphasis is on fresh, local ingredients, especially local oysters, shrimp, and fish. Like the dining room, the presentation is sophisticated but unpretentious, and the seafood is unapologetically fried. Why? Because fried fish, snapping-crisp on the outside and moist and tender on the inside, is good—really good, that's why, and Sundae Cafe happens to do it really well. Moreover, locals love fried fish but don't like to make it at home. For those who prefer not to indulge in a lot of fried food, the menu still features plenty of seafood that isn't from the fryer as well as a judicious selection of carefully prepared steaks, chops, and chicken. And even the fried fare is balanced with lighter accompaniments.

Double-Cut Pork Chop with Tybee Apple Chutney & Blue Cheese Bread Pudding

(SERVES 4)

For the chutney:

12 ounces (about 2–3) Granny Smith apples

¼ large yellow onion, chopped

1 tablespoon unsalted butter

1 tablespoon cider vinegar

½ cup (firmly packed) brown sugar

¼ teaspoon cinnamon

Dash of ground cayenne pepper

½ ounce (about 1 tablespoon) raisins

½ ounce (about 1 tablespoon) golden raisins

1 ounce (about 2 tablespoons) diced roasted red pepper

For the blue cheese bread pudding:

2 tablespoons (¼ stick) unsalted butter

½ medium green bell pepper, cored, seeded, and chopped

¼ large yellow onion, chopped

½ cup frozen whole kernel corn, thawed and drained

1 tablespoon seeded and diced jalapeño pepper

¾ cup heavy cream

1 large egg, lightly beaten

4 stale large buttermilk biscuits, coarsely crumbled

¾ cup crumbled blue cheese

Salt and freshly milled black pepper

For the pork chops:

4 double-cut bone-in pork chops

Salt and freshly milled black pepper

About ¼ cup hickory-smoke flavored barbecue sauce (Cattlemen's preferred)

Special Equipment: four flan dishes or custard cups

To make the chutney: Peel and slice the apples. In a heavy-bottomed pan, sauté the onion in the butter over medium heat for 2 minutes. Add the apples and cook, tossing, until tender. Add the vinegar and brown sugar and let it reduce 3 minutes, stirring often. Remove it from the heat and add the spices, raisins, and roasted pepper. Cool. This can be made ahead. Cover and refrigerate until needed. It will keep for up to 2 months.

To make the bread pudding: Position a rack in the center of the oven and preheat it to 350°F. Spray four metal individual flan dishes or custard cups with cooking spray. Put the butter in a large sauté pan or skillet over medium heat. When it is just melted, add the peppers and onions and sauté until they are softened but not browned, about 5 minutes. Stir in the corn and jalapeños and cook a minute longer. Turn off the heat and let it cool.

Beat together the cream and egg in a large mixing bowl. Stir in the crumbled biscuits and ½ cup cheese. Fold in the onion and pepper mixture, season with salt and pepper and pour the batter into the prepared dishes. Level the top with a spatula and top with the remaining cheese. Bake until golden brown on top and set at the center, about 18 minutes.

To make the pork chops: Prepare a grill with a medium-hot fire. Season the chops with salt and pepper. Grill, turning once, to an internal temperature of 140°F for medium. Remove them to a platter, brush with barbecue sauce, cover, and let rest 5 minutes before serving. Internal temperature will continue to rise while chops rest.

To serve: Unmold the bread puddings onto four warmed serving plates. Lay a chop to one side of the pudding, top with chutney, and serve at once.

Margarita Scallops

(SERVES 4)

For the black bean and corn salsa:

1 (28-ounce) can black beans, rinsed and drained

2 large ears corn, cooked (preferably grill-roasted), kernels cut from the cob

½ red onion, finely diced

Salt and cayenne pepper or hot sauce, to taste

1 bunch cilantro, chopped

1 teaspoon ground cumin

1 jalapeño pepper, cored, seeded, and diced small

Juice of 1 lime

For the roasted red pepper aioli:

1 (28-ounce) can roasted red peppers

2 cloves garlic, peeled and minced

1 cup mayonnaise

4 (6-inch) flour or corn tortillas, or 20 purchased flour or corn tortilla chips

Vegetable oil, if frying the tortilla chips

½ (6-ounce) can frozen orange juice concentrate, thawed

Juice of 1 lime

¼ cup tequila

1 bunch cilantro, chopped

Salt and freshly milled black pepper

20 large dry-pack sea scallops

Make the salsa: Combine all the salsa ingredients in a glass or stainless steel mixing bowl.

Make the aioli: Drain and finely chop the peppers. Blend with the garlic and mayonnaise, cover, and refrigerate until needed.

Cut each tortilla into 5 triangles. Half fill a deep fryer or deep, heavy-bottomed pot with oil and heat it to 360°F over medium-high heat. Fry the tortillas in batches until golden brown and crisp and drain them on paper towels. Set aside. (You may substitute purchased flour or corn tortilla chips.)

Combine the orange juice concentrate, lime juice, tequila, and cilantro in a large glass or stainless steel bowl that will comfortably hold the scallops. Season lightly with a pinch each of salt and pepper. Wipe the scallops dry and add them to the marinade, tossing to coat them. Marinate 10 to 15 minutes. Meanwhile, prepare a grill with a medium-hot fire. Remove the scallops from their marinade, wipe dry and grill about 2 to 3 minutes per side, until blackened and cooked through. Quickly arrange the tortilla chips on serving plates, allowing 5 per plate. Top each chip with a spoonful of black bean and corn salsa. Place 1 scallop over the salsa on each chip, spoon a little aioli over them, and serve at once.

Taco Abajo

217 1/2 West Broughton Street (cellar)
(912) 480-9050
www.tacoabajo.com
Managing Partner: Robert Hauft
Executive Chef: Donnie Simmons

Abajo is Spanish for "below"—and that's exactly where you'll find Taco Abajo—down a long flight of stairs in the basement of one of Broughton Street's restored nineteenth-century storefronts. Specializing in authentic Mexican street food, their slogan, "A taco truck—hold the wheels" nicely wraps up this casual, urban-hip restaurant and nightspot. Brash, colorful, and casual, with a game room, live entertainment, no less than ten flat-screen televisions, and full bar featuring a selection of tequila and craft beer that is longer than many a fine-dining wine list, Taco Abajo is young and invitingly laid-back. But if you're inclined to think of it as just another cheap taqueria dive for hungry students, think again. Abajo's classically trained chef, Donnie Simmons, takes his street food seriously, and brings to his cooking all the passion, care, and attention as if it were being presented on fine china at the starched and pressed tables of the most formal of restaurants.

Everything here is fresh and mostly local: Chef Donnie gets the majority of his produce from local organic growers—including the chile peppers that go into his house-

made salsas, from the illusive, legendary "ghost chiles" (reputed to be the hottest chile pepper on the planet) to the "seven-pot" peppers that are the foundation of his intensely spicy Death Sauce. The menu encompasses the usual popular street foods like tacos, burritos, and salads, but Chef Donnie also likes to shake things up with daily specials incorporating such exotica as ostrich, antelope, kangaroo, and elk, and regularly steps out of the box with sauces and salsas such as his roasted pear and poblano sauce and trademark Fig, Sweat, and Tears (a hot sauce made with local figs and chipotle peppers), adding a contemporary flair to the Mexican tradition. To keep things lively, he also offers special limited-seating dinners a couple of times each month, where he gets to set aside the Mexican theme altogether and present his take on cuisines from all over the world, rounded out by pairings with fine wines or, where appropriate, craft beers from the restaurant's extensive collection.

Open weekdays from eleven in the morning until they're "damned good and ready" to close, Taco Abajo stays open even later on weekends with live entertainment that keeps the place hopping until the wee hours.

Cilantro Lime Shrimp Tacos

(SERVES 6)

¼ cup freshly squeezed lime juice

¼ cup chopped fresh cilantro

¼ teaspoon garlic powder

¼ teaspoon ground coriander

½ teaspoon kosher salt

30 medium shrimp, peeled, deveined, and tails off

6 (6-inch) soft flour or corn tortillas

2 cups chopped napa cabbage

½ fresh lime

About 1 tablespoon olive oil

2 radishes, thinly sliced

8 ounces (1 cup) plain sour cream, or 4 ounces (½ cup) seasoned sour cream (see Note below), or 1 cup guacamole

Combine the lime juice, cilantro, garlic powder, coriander, and salt in large bowl. Add the shrimp, stir to combine, and then cover and refrigerate for no more than 30 minutes (longer and you will begin to "cook" the shrimp like a seviche).

Heat the tortillas according to manufacturer's directions. Lay them flat and top with napa cabbage. Warm 1 tablespoon olive oil in a nonstick sauté pan over medium high heat and add the shrimp. Sauté, tossing constantly, until pink and loosely curled. Just before removing them from the heat, squeeze half a fresh lime over the shrimp, being careful to catch any seeds from the lime. Remove the pan from heat and place 5 shrimp on each taco, lay down 5 or 6 radish slices on each taco, then dress with sour cream or guacamole. Fold the tacos and serve immediately.

Note: For added flavor, you may add 2 tablespoons ground coriander, 1 tablespoon garlic powder, and the juice from half a lime to ½ cup sour cream, stir well, and use it in place of plain sour cream. Because its flavor is more pronounced, you will need less of it.

Sweet Seasoned Fried Corn on the Cob

(SERVES 6)

Another popular specialty of Taco Abajo is one of the great, classic Mexican street foods—spiced deep fried corn on the cob.

6 fresh ears corn

1 quart whole milk

Canola oil, for frying

2 tablespoons dark brown sugar

1 tablespoons ground coriander

1 teaspoon kosher salt

1 teaspoon cracked black pepper

¾ cup mayonnaise (Chef Donnie prefers Duke's)

About ¼ cup chopped fresh cilantro for serving (optional)

Shuck and then break or cut the ears of corn crosswise into 4- to 5-inch-long pieces. Place them in a casserole dish, pour milk over them and refrigerate for 4 hours, rotating the corn every hour. Remove it from the refrigerator and let it sit at room temperature for an hour. Pour off the milk and pat the corn dry with paper towels.

Half fill a deep fryer or deep, wide pot with oil (at least 2 inches deep but no more than halfway up the sides) and heat it to 350°F. Meanwhile, combine the brown sugar, coriander, salt, pepper, and mayonnaise, blending well, and put it into a flat, low-sided pan, such as a jelly roll pan.

When the oil is hot, fry the corn in batches until the kernels begin to turn golden brown or caramel colored. Remove the corn from fryer with tongs and roll it in the mayonnaise mixture. If preferred, sprinkle it with chopped cilantro and serve at once.

Guacamole Abajo

(MAKES ABOUT 4 CUPS)

4 cups avocado pulp (6–8 fresh avocados depending on size)

¼ cup diced red onion

¼ cup chopped fresh cilantro

¼ cup fresh lime juice

2 tablespoons seeded and finely diced jalapeño

½ teaspoon salt

Cut the avocados in half, remove the pits, and scoop the pulp into a large mixing bowl. Add remaining ingredients and blend thoroughly by hand. The guacamole can be coarse or creamy: if you prefer it creamier, just blend longer.

Tangerine Fusion + Sushi Bar

11215 Abercorn Street
(912) 920-5504
www.tangerinefusion.com
Chef/Owner: Ele Tran
Executive Chef: Sean Thongsiri

Until recently, Savannah's fine-dining scene was confined to its historic downtown, where a regular stream of visitors could be depended upon to supplement local patronage. And yet, the lion's share of Savannah's population is found on its barrier islands and in the many suburban neighborhoods of the sprawling Southside, which have traditionally been landscaped with strip shopping centers, drive-through fast-food joints, and chain restaurants. Until recently, the Southside had very few options for fine dining, and almost none (beyond the occasional Latino grocery and taqueria) for really authentic ethnic cuisines.

Fortunately that has begun to change in the last decade as adventurous restaurateurs begin to branch out from downtown. A notable example of this is Tangerine Fusion, which can be found in an ordinary strip center at the edge of Southside's Windsor Forest neighborhood. This suave little Pan-Asian restaurant may look, on the outside, like most of the other shopping-center cafes that line Abercorn Extension, but inside, it is anything but ordinary. Its walls are vibrant with its namesake color, and the crisp white linens on its tables are accented by napkins that match those walls and by fresh tropical flowers. Intimate, curtained booths that line its open dining room, an elegantly appointed, fully stocked bar, and sleek, modern lighting all create an atmosphere that is at once cozy and sophisticated. The servers, like Nancy (shown left), give personality to Tangerine.

Air fragrant with garlic and ginger suggests a menu that is an equally sophisticated fusion of Pan-Asian cookery. The cuisines of Vietnam, Thailand, Cambodia, and Laos are seamlessly blended together, sprinkled with a few Western standards such as pan-seared prime filet steak with red wine reduction, and rounded out by a full a la carte selection of fresh sushi and sashimi. The presentations, like the cooking, are as elegant and lovely as they are simple and unpretentious.

Sweet Basil Chicken with Scallions

(SERVES 4)

2 large or 4 small boneless, skinless chicken breasts
4 teaspoons oyster sauce
4 teaspoons fish sauce
4 teaspoons sugar
4 teaspoons chile paste
4 teaspoons coconut milk
4 teaspoons cooking oil
4 teaspoons crushed, minced garlic
4 small green scallions, sliced on the diagonal into
    1-inch lengths
2 cups prepared and sliced vegetables such as bamboo
    shoots, white or yellow onion, white mushrooms,
    snow peas, red bell peppers
About ¼ cup (well packed) small Thai or other sweet
    basil leaves
Lettuce leaves, for serving
Cilantro sprigs, for garnish (optional)
4 cups hot steamed aromatic rice, such as jasmine

Cut the chicken across the grain into thin slices.
Combine the oyster sauce, fish sauce, sugar,
chile paste, and coconut milk in a small bowl.
Heat a wok over high heat. Drizzle in the oil, add
the garlic, and toss until hot.

Add the chicken and stir-fry until it loses its
raw, pink color, then add the combined sauce
ingredients and cook for about 2 minutes. Add
the scallions and desired vegetables and stir fry
for another 2 to 3 minutes. Add the basil and
toss well.

Line four serving plates with lettuce leaves,
divide the chicken among them, and garnish with
cilantro, if desired. Serve at once with rice.

THE TEA ROOM

7 EAST BROUGHTON STREET
(912) 239-9690
WWW.SAVANNAHTEAROOM.COM
OWNERS: BECKY WRIGHT AND ELIZABETH RUBY
CHEF: ANDRE BAXTER

Right in the middle of bustling Broughton Street is a quiet little haven where time slows down and takes the pace of a calmer, gentler era, a place where visitors and locals alike go to lunch and reflect while sipping perfectly brewed tea from delicate china cups. A downtown fixture since December 1997, The Tea Room, owned by dynamic mother-daughter team Becky Wright and Elizabeth Ruby, is genteel yet not in the least fussy, refined and yet relaxed and casual.

The front of the house is a small retail space where an impressive variety of exceptionally fine tea leaves are sold by the ounce. Dominated by a tall Arts and Crafts–style case filled with polished metal canisters of tea, it has the feel of an old-fashioned English tea shop, but vintage and modern tea paraphernalia, books on tea, and Elizabeth Ruby's uniquely designed handmade jewelry lend a personal touch and make it distinctly contemporary.

Of the three dining areas, all decorated in the style of Arts and Crafts–era designer Charles Rennie Mackintosh, the most popular is without doubt the Library. Set off by vintage pocket doors, this cozy, softly lit room features a working fireplace surrounded by a pair of deep wing chairs and a large ottoman scattered with magazines and newspapers, giving it the feel of a library in an English country house at the turn of the century.

Wright and Ruby credit their success mainly to "sheer stubborn tenacity," but a lot is owed to their charm and to the talents of Chef Andre Baxter, who has been with them since they opened. His shortbread has become almost legendary in Savannah, and his daily soups and chef's specials keep locals coming back more than once a week.

Never content to have just one menu, Chef Andre regularly changes it with his mood and with the season. One thing, however, has never changed: the signature Lapsang chicken salad. Made with chicken poached in smoky Lapsang tea, it has a delicately smoked, almost barbecued flavor that has made it their most popular dish and most-asked-for recipe.

LAPSANG-POACHED CHICKEN SALAD

(SERVES 8)

4 large boneless, skinless chicken breasts

½ cup plus 2 tablespoons soy sauce

4 tablespoons Lapsang tea leaves

2 tablespoons small-dice red bell pepper

2 tablespoons small-dice yellow bell pepper

1 Granny Smith apple, cored and diced small

1 clove garlic, lightly crushed and minced

1⅛ teaspoons salt

¼ teaspoon freshly milled pepper

1¼ teaspoons ground ginger

1 cup mayonnaise

4 cups small leaf lettuce, if serving as a salad,
    or 4 small handfuls if making sandwiches

16 slices sandwich bread of your choice,
    for serving (optional)

Rinse the chicken breasts and pat them dry. Trim away any excess fat and cartilage and put them in a 3-quart saucepan. Completely cover with cold water and add ½ cup soy sauce and 2 tablespoons tea leaves. Turn on the heat to medium low and bring slowly to a simmer. Reduce the heat to a bare simmer and poach 30 minutes. Turn off the heat and let cool.

While the chicken is cooling, combine both bell peppers and the apple in a mixing bowl and pour the remaining soy sauce over them. Add the garlic and remaining 2 tablespoons tea. Set it aside.

Roughly chop the chicken and fold it into the pepper and apple mixture. Add the salt, pepper, ginger, and mayonnaise, and gently but thoroughly mix to combine. Refrigerate until needed and serve cold.

The salad can be scooped onto a bed of lettuce leaves and served plain, or spread onto a slice of sandwich bread, topped with the lettuce and a second slice of bread. Cut diagonally into halves if serving for lunch, or quarters for afternoon tea, and serve at once.

THRIVE A CARRY OUT CAFE

4700 US HIGHWAY 80 EAST
(WHITMARSH ISLAND ON THE WAY TO TYBEE BEACH)
(912) 898-2131
WWW.THRIVEACARRYOUTCAFE.COM
CHEF/OWNER: WENDY ARMSTRONG

In a bustling island shopping center just a few doors down from Wiley's Championship BBQ (page 178), the self-proclaimed "home of naughty food," is another storefront cafe that one could say is its exact polar opposite: Thrive. This immaculate little take-out emporium, with sunny yellow walls and deli cases filled with platters of colorful, irresistible fresh-daily prepared foods, is all about things that only taste naughty. Passing the thriving

little herb garden in the parking lot out front, you know you're not going into just any take-out sandwich joint. Specializing in fresh, local ingredients, thoughtfully and carefully prepared, Thrive is Savannah's first and only green-certified restaurant, which means that not only are the food products it serves organic or naturally raised, the entire operation, from energy use to take-out containers, are environmentally conscious.

"I grew up in Vermont," jokes Thrive's chef/owner, Wendy Armstrong, a lovely, energetic young woman with a warm, ready smile, "so of course that makes me a bit of a tree hugger!"

Chef Armstrong is far more than an ardent environmentalist, however: She's a passionate cook who firmly believes the old adage that "we are what we eat." All the same, when she first came to Savannah, it was to study art at SCAD, with no thought of cooking professionally. But while she fell in love with the city, she soon realized that her talents lay in a different kind of art, so she left to study the culinary arts at the Fort Lauderdale Art Institute. Always eager to expand her own knowledge and skill, she's also taken courses of study at the Culinary Institute in New York and, during a fourteen-year stint as a yacht chef, in such far-flung places as Florence, Italy, and southern Mexico.

In all those years on a boat, however, she says she never forgot about Savannah, and it tugged at her heartstrings. "I knew that when I wanted to live on land again, I'd have to come back here."

When she eventually did return, the one thing that was missing was easy access to food that was locally and naturally grown yet still affordable. Changing that became her mission, and while the concept for Thrive was not new when it opened in 2008, it was new to Savannah. Chef Armstrong is pleased that a lively local food culture has emerged in the area since then, with a network of businesses that support and feed one another. Her list of vendors could almost be an index for this book—seafood from Charles J. Russo's (page 44), produce from Greenbridge Farm, beef from Hunter Cattle Company (page 85), pasta from FraLi Gourmet (page 156), and cheesecakes from FORM (page 77)—just to name a few.

Keeping the food affordable is a challenge for the business, says Chef Armstrong. "Because of the kind of products we use, our margins are pretty tight. But it's very satisfying to think that we're educating and making a difference in the community."

WILD GEORGIA SHRIMP & CUCUMBER SALAD

(SERVES 6–8)

1 teaspoon Old Bay Seasoning

1 lemon, halved (½ cut into wedges)

1 large cucumber, preferably organic

1 red bell pepper, preferably organic

½ cup light mayonnaise

½ teaspoon Sriracha sauce (garlic-chile hot sauce), or to taste

1 teaspoon relish (your choice)

Chopped flat-leaf parsley, preferably organic

3 pounds local Georgia wild-caught shrimp, peeled and deveined

Halved avocados or toast, for serving

Bring a large pot of water to a boil. Season it with Old Bay and the juice from half of the lemon. Meanwhile split, seed, and dice the cucumber and pepper into ½-inch pieces and set them aside. Blend together the mayonnaise, Sriracha, relish, and a little of the parsley, to taste. Set this aside as well.

Prepare a large bowl with crushed ice. Drop the shrimp into the seasoned boiling water, watching carefully because shrimp cook quickly. When they begin to float to the top and appear pink in color (about 1 to 2 minutes), drain and put them in the crushed ice, stirring, to arrest the cooking. Remove them from the ice when cold.

In a large mixing bowl mix together the cucumber, pepper, dressing, and shrimp, gently folding with a rubber spatula or your hands to avoid breaking the shrimp. Garnish with the lemon wedges and a sprinkling of fresh parsley. Serve on halved avocados or toast.

CURRIED SWEET POTATO SOUP

(SERVES 4)

1½ pounds sweet potatoes

Sea salt

Olive oil

Honey

½ cup coconut milk

1 cup vegetable stock

1 tablespoon dark brown sugar

1 tablespoon red curry paste

Sea salt

Wash, peel, and cut the sweet potatoes in half. Put them in a pot, completely cover them with water, and bring it to a boil over medium high heat. Reduce the heat to a simmer and cook until the potatoes are tender.

Drain, let cool slightly, and put them in a mixing bowl or into the bowl of a food processor. Season lightly with salt, a drizzle of olive oil, and a little honey, all to taste, and whip them to a puree with a mixer or the food processor. You will need 2 cups puree. Set aside any excess for another use.

Put the puree, coconut milk, stock, sugar, curry, and a pinch of salt together in a blender or food processor and blend until smooth. Adjust seasonings and thickness, thinning with water or stock if necessary. Serve warm or chilled.

Vic's on the River

26 East Bay Street (above Factor's Walk next to City Hall)
(912) 721-1000
WWW.VICSONTHERIVER.COM
Owners: Bill Hall and Irving Victor
Executive Chef: Brian Hanson

Just over a jasmine-covered iron footbridge spanning Factor's Walk to the east of City Hall is a stately mid-nineteenth-century brick building whose tall, wide arched windows overlook both Bay Street and Savannah's bustling Riverfront. Built in 1858 by John Norris, architect for the imposing granite Customs House directly across the street and a number of Savannah's most elegant mansions, its generous proportions and handsome detailing make it appear to have been destined for something far more elegant than its original purpose as a cotton broker's office and warehouse—something exactly like Vic's on the River, the upscale restaurant that now calls it home.

Formerly called The River Grill, the restaurant moved to its present location and reopened in January of 2006 as Vic's on the River, co-owner Bill Hall's surprise tribute to his business partner, Dr. Irving Victor. Affectionately known around Savannah as "Doctor Vic," this snow-haired urologist with a passion for cooking and cookbook collecting shared Hall's vision for a beautiful restaurant where locals could eat well yet affordably. They met that vision architecturally by respecting the rich history of the building with an understated decor. When they found a map drawn by Union soldiers who were billeted in the building during Sherman's occupation, they took steps to conserve it and make it a part of the decorations.

At the table, they met the vision by offering traditional Southern-style fare made with fresh, regional ingredients and a bit of a continental accent. For example, crab cakes accompanied by a spicy mayonnaise-based sauce are an old local favorite, and even though rice is no longer grown in the region, it is to Savannahians what pasta is to Italians. In Vic's Jumbo Crab Cakes with Pesto Risotto and Roasted Red Pepper Aioli, all those traditional foods—crab, spicy sauce, and rice—are present, but reinterpreted in a way that is decidedly not tradition bound.

Vic's Jumbo Crab Cakes with Pesto Risotto & Roasted Red Pepper Aioli

(SERVES 6)

For the roasted red pepper aioli (makes about 1½ cups):

2 egg yolks
3 cloves roasted garlic, peeled (see Note)
1 teaspoon red wine vinegar
⅓ teaspoon Dijon mustard
1 tablespoon lemon juice
1 roasted red pepper, peeled (see Note)
⅔ cup olive or vegetable oil
Salt and freshly milled pepper, to taste

For the crab cakes:

2 large eggs
½ cup mayonnaise
1 tablespoon Dijon mustard
1 tablespoon Worcestershire sauce
1 tablespoon Old Bay Seasoning
2 tablespoons chopped parsley
Dash of Tabasco Sauce, to taste
2 pounds jumbo lump crabmeat
1 cup panko bread crumbs
Salt and freshly milled black pepper

For the pesto (makes about 1 cup):

1 loosely packed cup fresh basil leaves
2 cloves garlic, chopped
¼ cup toasted pine nuts
¼ cup shredded Parmigiano Reggiano
⅛ cup olive oil
Salt

For the risotto:

8 ounces unsalted butter
2 yellow onions, chopped
2 cups raw arborio rice
1 cup dry white wine
5 cups chicken broth
½ cups freshly grated Parmigiano Reggiano
2 tablespoons (¼ stick) unsalted butter, softened
Salt and freshly milled black pepper

Vegetable oil, for sautéeing the crab cakes

Make the aioli: Put the egg yolks, roasted garlic, vinegar, mustard, lemon juice, and pepper in the work bowl of a food processor fitted with a steel blade. Blend well.

With the motor running, slowly add the oil in a thin steady stream. The motor sound will change and sound more "hollow" as the sauce emulsifies. Season with salt and pepper to taste. Transfer to a storage container, cover well, and refrigerate until needed.

Make the crab cakes: Break the eggs into a large mixing bowl and lightly beat them. Add the mayonnaise, mustard, Worcestershire, Old Bay, parsley, and a dash or so of Tabasco, to taste, and mix well. Fold in the crabmeat and panko and season to taste with salt and pepper.

Mold the mixture into 12 (3-ounce) cakes. Let rest in the refrigerator for 20 minutes to an hour.

Make the pesto: Combine the basil, garlic, pine nuts, Parmigiano, and oil in a food processor and blend for 1 minute. Taste and season with salt as needed.

Make the risotto: In a large saucepan melt the butter over medium heat and sauté the onions until translucent. Add the rice and continue to cook for 5 minutes, stirring frequently. Add the white wine and cook until absorbed. Now add chicken stock 1 cup at a time, stirring almost constantly, until rice is al dente (not mushy) and creamy, about 20 minutes.

Off the heat, stir in the Parmigiano and butter, taste, and season to taste with salt and pepper. (The risotto can also be served as is, without adding the pesto.) To finish it with pesto, combine the risotto and pesto before adding salt and pepper and mix well. Taste and adjust seasonings.

Film a large, heavy-bottomed skillet with oil and heat over medium heat. Sauté the crab cakes, in batches if necessary, until golden brown on all sides and set, about 4 to 5 minutes per side.

To serve: Divide the risotto among six heated serving plates. Arrange 2 crab cakes per plate, slightly overlapping the risotto, dot the plate with red pepper aioli, and serve immediately.

Notes: To roast garlic, preheat the oven to 400°F. Cut ¼-inch from the top (stem end) of a whole head of garlic and lay it on a piece of foil. Drizzle with olive oil, wrap the foil around it, lay it on a small rimmed pan and bake until the garlic is softened, about 45 minutes. (Any leftover roasted garlic will keep in the refrigerator, well-wrapped or in a covered container, for up to four days.) To roast red pepper, lay it on a rimmed sheet pan and roast, turning occasionally, at 450°F until the skin blackens. Put the pepper into a paper bag, close it, and let it sit 15 minutes, then peel away the blackened skin, core, and seed the pepper.

WILEY'S CHAMPIONSHIP BBQ

4700 US HIGHWAY 80 EAST
(WHITMARSH ISLAND ON THE WAY TO TYBEE BEACH)
(912) 201-3259
WWW.WILEYSCHAMPIONSHIPBBQ.COM
OWNERS: WILEY AND JANET MCCRARY

Visitors who whiz by this little storefront cafe, located in a strip shopping center on the way to Tybee Beach, might be inclined to think its name a bit braggadocio, if not pretentious, but the fact is, "championship" in this instance is no empty boast. Owners Wiley and Janet McCrary have garnered just about every barbecue competition award that can be had, from both the Memphis and Kansas City competition circuits. This little 'cue joint, with bright red walls plastered with awards, the atmosphere of a neighborhood pub, and air reassuringly tinged with the aroma of hardwood smoke, is where you'll find some of the best ribs, brisket, and pulled pork in the area, if not Georgia.

"This is not a health food store," quips Wiley McCrary from his customary stool at the lunch counter, cigar in his hand, gravel in his voice, and a twinkle in his eye, "We're the home of naughty food."

That may be why it's so irresistible.

Wiley's is the fulfillment of a long-term dream of the McCrarys to move to Savannah, slow down, and scale back with a smaller version of the barbecue catering business they'd had in Atlanta. As it has turned out, however, the only scaling back they've been able to accomplish is the size of the dining room: The place is tiny, but its booming business has kept the McCrarys busier than ever.

It's their own fault: The flavors here are as big, bold, and addictive as the place is small. Aside from award-worthy pork, beef, and chicken barbecue, there's the "Better than Sex" finishing sauce, fried pickles, sweet potato fries that are actually crisp, old-fashioned slow-cooked collards, and daily specials that aren't always from the pit. All of that keeps this little 'cue joint packed with locals and visitors alike.

A favorite appetizer with Wiley's regulars is Redneck Nachos, a sinfully addictive concoction of house-made potato chips hot from the fryer topped with pulled pork barbecue, cheddar sauce, jalapeños, and a touch of that signature Better than Sex sauce.

Redneck Nachos

(SERVES 4–8, DEPENDING ON APPETITES)

1½ pounds potatoes, peeled and thinly sliced on a mandoline, for chips

Oil, for frying

10 ounces shredded white cheddar

1 generous cup heavy cream

About 14 ounces barbecued pork shoulder, pulled

About 1 small jar sliced pickled jalapeño peppers, to taste (you may not use all of them)

About ½ cup Wiley's Better than Sex barbecue sauce (see Note), or your favorite

Wipe the potato chips dry. Put enough oil in a deep fryer or deep, heavy-bottomed dutch oven to come halfway up the sides and heat it to 350°F to 365°F. While the oil is heating, combine the cheddar and cream in a pan or microwave-safe dish (Wiley's does the latter) and heat, whisking occasionally, until it is melted and smooth. Turn off the heat but keep warm.

When the oil is hot, fry the chips in small batches until browned and crisp. Drain each batch on paper towels and keep warm.

To serve, spread the chips on individual plates or paper-lined baskets. Sprinkle generously with the pulled pork, drizzle with cheese sauce, scatter jalapeños over the top, and dot with barbecue sauce, all to taste. Serve immediately.

Note: Wiley's Better than Sex barbecue sauce, which comes in two versions, original and "extra tingly," is sold at the restaurant, online at www.wileyschampionshipbbq.com, and at a few local retailers.

WRIGHT SQUARE CAFE

21 WEST YORK STREET (AT WRIGHT SQUARE)
(912) 238-1150
WWW.WRIGHTSQUARECAFE.COM
OWNER: GARY HALL

Just south of Broughton Street on Bull is Wright Square, the center green for one of the four original wards laid out by Oglethorpe himself. Locals call this shady, camellia-studded park "courthouse square," since it is defined to the west by the ornate marble edifice of the Federal Courthouse and to the east by the Romanesque Revival Chatham County Courthouse and Lutheran Church of the Ascension, a tangible reminder of heavenly law. One of Savannah's most historically significant squares, it's also a thriving retail hub filled with art galleries, boutique shops, and, just off its southwest corner, a little cafe of the same name, where locals and visitors alike stop to lunch, take a late morning coffee break, or indulge in a midafternoon chocolate fix.

When owner Gary Hall first opened the Wright Square Cafe in October of 2001, barely a month after the cataclysmic events of 9/11, he had no idea that his unassuming take-out shop and outlet for handmade chocolates and then hard-to-find specialty foods would become a community institution. Within just a few years, however, the dining area had to be doubled to accommodate the lunch crowds, and in 2009, professional chocolatier Adam Turoni (page 52) came on board, taking the house-made chocolates to a whole new level.

Although the house-made chocolates, prominently displayed at the front of the food service area, are Hall's passion, he believes the cafe's enduring success is owed more to the everyday food displayed around the corner from them—the likes of old-fashioned curried chicken salad; bright, marinated vegetable salads; an array of unusual sandwich wraps, seasonal soups and chili; and an irresistible assortment of homemade cookies, dessert bars, and pastries. But he also believes a large part of the success is due to a long-term staff that tends to treat the place as their own and the customers as extended family. With a fond smile he explains, "We encourage that feeling of ownership, and love the way they cut up with the customers."

Baked Chicken Wrap
with Fig Caramelized Onions

(SERVES 6)

Of all the cafe's offerings, by far the most popular is the Herb-Baked Chicken Wrap with Fig Caramelized Onions, which has been on the menu ever since the place opened. The key element is a simple conserve of onions caramelized with fig jam. You'll find yourself wanting to prepare it in double batches, since it not only makes this sandwich sing, but is also a fine condiment for just about any roasted meat or poultry.

For the herb baked chicken:

3 boneless, skinless chicken breasts
1 teaspoon each dried rosemary, oregano, and basil
¼ cup olive oil
Salt and freshly milled black pepper

For the fig caramelized onions:

½ tablespoon unsalted butter
1½–2 cups thinly sliced yellow onions
⅓ cup fig preserves

For finishing the wrap:

6 flour tortillas
About ¼–½ cup cream cheese, softened
About 3 cups shredded lettuce
About 1½ cups diced ripe tomato
1 cup crumbled feta
6 tablespoons pecan pieces

Special Equipment: **panini press or cast-iron skillet and grill press**

Cut the chicken breasts into ½-inch strips and put them in a glass or stainless steel bowl with the herbs, olive oil, and salt and pepper to taste. Toss until well mixed, cover, and marinate in the refrigerator for 1 hour.

Remove from the refrigerator 30 minutes before cooking, and preheat the oven to 350°F.

Spread the chicken on a rimmed baking sheet and bake, turning once, until it is just cooked through, about 20 minutes, depending on the thickness. Let cool.

Melt the butter in a skillet or sauté pan over medium heat. Add the onions and sauté, tossing often, until they're golden brown, about 5 to 8 minutes. Stir in the fig preserves, raise the heat, and stir until the preserves reduce and thicken, just before the sugars caramelize. Turn off the heat.

To assemble the wrap: Lay a tortilla flat on a work surface. Lightly smear it with a little cream cheese around the edge of the top half of the tortilla (this will help hold the wrap together). Put a handful of lettuce and spoonful of tomato in the center. Top with a couple of chicken breast strips and spread about 1½ to 2 tablespoons of the fig caramelized onions over it. Sprinkle with feta and pecans and tightly roll the wrap from the bottom side up, trying to get most of the air pockets out of it as you go.

Heat an electric or stovetop panini press or a cast-iron skillet and grill press. Place the wrap in the press, close the press (or weight the sandwich with the heated press) and heat until warm and the tortilla is lightly toasted.

Zunzi's

108 East York Street
(912) 443-9555
www.zunzis.com
Chefs/Owners: Gabriella and John De Beer

Ever since its founding, Savannah's historic downtown has been dotted with small yet lively out-of-the-way spots where unusual food and drink can be found, from Tondee's Tavern, haunt of the Sons of Liberty at the beginning of the Revolution, to back-alley barbecue joints, to modern-day take-out shops, all run by a real international assortment of folks. One of the liveliest and most interesting of these today is Zunzi's, a diminutive take-out shop that can be found beneath a bright display of American and South African flags that hang from the York Street side of an old row house between the busy thoroughfares of Drayton and Abercorn.

Owners Gabriella and Johnny De Beer personify the international melting pot of Savannah's old downtown: She grew up in Switzerland with an Italian mother while he hails from South Africa. And the fare they offer reflects the happy collision between their differing culinary backgrounds, a rich blending of Italian, South African, Indian, and

American cookery. You'll find lasagna right next to spicy house-made South African sausages, curries right beside burgers, Middle Eastern–style wraps nestled up to unique American-style sandwiches filled with unusual combinations like ham, cheese, and asparagus. Long a favorite with locals, Zunzi's was catapulted into the national limelight when one of those sandwiches was featured on Adam Richman's popular Travel Channel program *Best Sandwich in America*. Dubbed The Conquistador, it's a French roll thickly stuffed with house-baked chicken.

Johnny, a charmingly handsome, gregarious fellow who makes the most of his South African lilt as the tireless front man for the business, obviously loves the interaction with customers as he presses newcomers with samples and jokes with regulars. Gabriella, who prefers staying behind the scenes, is happy to let him be the spokesman and philosophically shrugs off Zunzi's recent celebrity. "I like flying under the radar. You know, we never did do any advertising. You like what I have, you'll come—if you don't, you'll go somewhere else. It's okay with me."

Not surprisingly, Gabriella goes her own way in the kitchen, as well, and does not like to measure anything; she "measures" instead with her tongue, tasting, and emphasizes that all the amounts given here should vary according to your own palate. "I believe if you want to cook something, you got to throw some things in and figure it out."

ZUNZI'S CURRY STEW

(SERVES 4)

1½ pounds stewing beef, preferably chuck,
    cut into 1-inch cubes
2 large cloves garlic, peeled and minced,
    to taste
Salt
4 large carrots, peeled and sliced
4 medium waxy boiling potatoes, peeled and cut into
    large chunks
About ¼ cup ketchup, to taste
About 1 hot chile pepper, seeded and minced, to taste
About ¼ teaspoon hot pepper flakes, to taste
About 1 teaspoon ground cumin, to taste
About 1 tablespoon curry powder or curry paste,
    to taste
1 cup fresh, frozen, or canned green peas (optional)
Sugar
Whole black pepper in a mill
Hot cooked rice, for serving (optional)

Put the beef and garlic in a heavy-bottomed dutch oven or pot and sprinkle with a large pinch of salt. Add enough water to cover the beef, bring it to a simmer, and simmer, covered, for 1 hour.

Add the carrots, potatoes, ketchup, and spices to taste. If it seems too thin, add a little more ketchup until it is thick enough to suit you, keeping in mind that it will also affect the flavor. Raise the heat, return the liquid to a boil, reduce the heat, and simmer, covered, until the beef is fork tender, about an hour longer. If desired, you may add peas to the stew, putting them in just before it's done and allowing about 20 minutes for fresh, 10 minutes for frozen, or 5 minutes for canned peas.

If the stew isn't thick enough, raise the heat briefly and let it cool down. Taste and adjust the salt and add sugar or pepper as needed (the former if you need to tone the spiciness down, the latter if it's not spicy enough to suit). Serve in thick bowls with rice if desired.

Recipe Index

General Index

About the Author

Damon Lee Fowler is a culinary historian, cooking teacher, food writer, and the author of six cookbooks, including *Classical Southern Cooking, Fried Chicken: The World's Best Recipes, Damon Lee Fowler's New Southern Kitchen, New Southern Baking,* and *The Savannah Cookbook.* His work has appeared in a number of national publications, including *Bon Appétit, Food & Wine,* and *Relish.* He is the featured food writer for the *Savannah Morning News.*

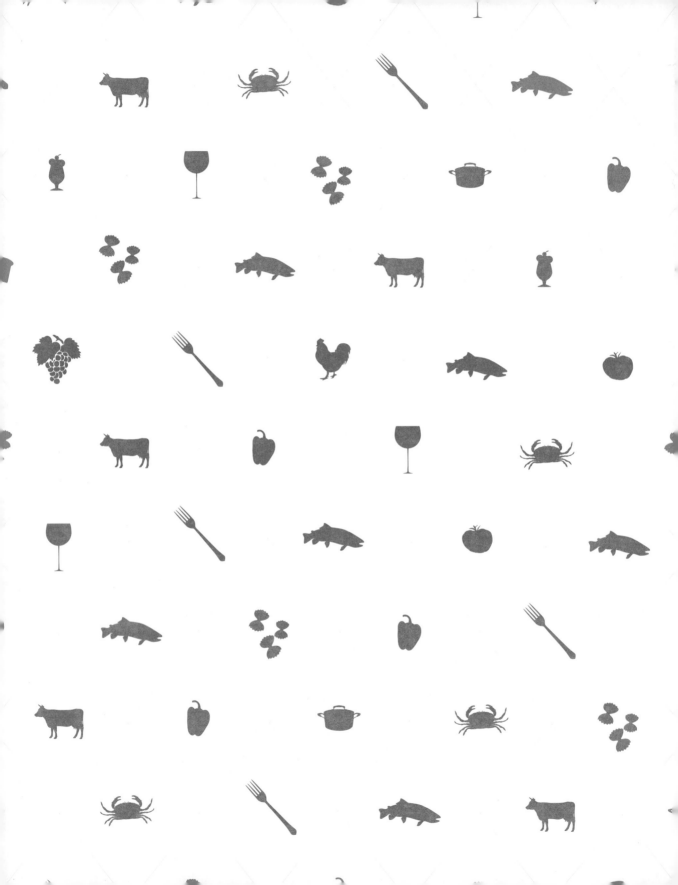